THE HAPPY READER
Issue nº 6 — Spring 2016

PART 1

Searching for time, the bright buzz of spri[ng, the]
world view of ETHAN HAWKE.

Finding the time 5
Snippets 6
The Interview: ETHAN HAWKE 8
   by Sadie Stein — *An exhilarating exchange with the readerly and writerly actor*
Ethan's spring reads 31

PART 2

The Book of the Season is Selma Lagerlöf's THE SAGA OF GÖSTA BERLING, with cinematic Sweden, band name boo-boos, ludic whirrings and lupine stirrings.

Introduction: Deeply Swedish 35
   by Seb Emina
Nature: A killer return. 36
   by Elin Unnes — *There are wolves in the woods again*
Society: 'This is a huge surprise!' 44
   by Nicholas Lezard — *The Nobel Prizes are very Swedish*
The other UK 46
Food & drink: Where the customer is always wrong. . . . 47
   by Travis Elborough — *We're a liquor store, so please go away*
Music: Why bands have the most ridiculous names 49
   by Simon Price — *Curiosity should've killed the band name*
Never-ending playtime. 52
   by Naomi Alderman — *Swap your cuckoo for a harlequin*
Icon: Fabricating Garbo 54
   by Yelena Moskovich — *Why Hollywood's ultimate star eventually vanished from public life*
Letters 61
In summer 62

Image: Courtesy of Svenskt Tenn

A pattern by celebrated Swedish designer Josef Frank (1885–1967). This pattern from the 1940s, more abstract than the floral motifs he was generally known for, was directly inspired by Jackson Pollock.

Having noticed fewer and fewer people reading paper books on the New York subway, Reinier Gerritsen decided to take a photograph each time he saw one. The result is a — nonetheless vast — portrait series entitled *The Last Book*.

THE HAPPY READER

FINDING THE TIME

The average adult reading speed is 300 words per minute, a rate at which Leo Tolstoy's *Anna Karenina* will take up twenty hours (give or take) of your time. The same maths allows two and a half hours for F. Scott Fitzgerald's *The Great Gatsby*, ten hours for Charlotte Brontë's *Jane Eyre*, and a mountainous ninety-eight hours for all five of George R. R. Martin's *A Song of Ice and Fire* (aka *Game of Thrones*) novels.

Of course these calculations are, in almost all ways, pointless. They reduce a rich and varied experience to the most daunting of time data, and actually tell us nothing practical. Who reads anything at a consistent speed anyway? Books are not movies; they don't have a running time. We read some sentences more quickly than others; our reasons for doing so are as varied as books themselves. I can spend ten minutes on a paragraph because I am bored, or because I want to savour every word. I can power through a hundred pages in an hour because I am thrilled, or because it is the song-filled Tom Bombadil section of *The Lord of the Rings*, and I just want it to — *'Hey! Come merry dol! derry dol! My darling!'* — be over.

Still, an anxiety for the modern reader is: where do I find these huge chunks of time? Between eating, working, and maintaining the glossy veneer of our online personas, it feels like we've never lived in busier times. A technology company made headlines once by claiming to have solved all this with a screen-based reading method granting the user a rate of 1,000 words per minute. Simply press 'play' and watch as one word after another pops up in quick succession (the weird trick: selected letters are highlighted in red to help the brain make sense of the flow). Perhaps books *can* have a running time: let's all go to the cinema and watch a six-hour screening of the 349,736 words that constitute *Anna Karenina*!

It's hard not to see this as productivity at the expense of pleasure. When a book takes hold of us it expands to fill any and all of the time that's available. On the train, sure, but also in the four minutes before our lunch date arrives, or the two minutes our electric toothbrush is active: it's the thing we turn to, our safe place — not an interlude from the day, but its very atmosphere. Ten or twenty or ninety hours isn't daunting, but exciting. Charge through this issue of *The Happy Reader* in an hour, or dwell on it for a year: we promise not to judge.

THE HAPPY READER
Bookish Quarterly
Issue nº 6 — Spring 2016

The Happy Reader is a collaboration between Penguin Books and Fantastic Man

EDITOR-IN-CHIEF
Seb Emina

EDITORIAL DIRECTORS
Jop van Bennekom
Gert Jonkers

MANAGING EDITOR
Cecilia Stein

DESIGN
Matthew Young

DESIGN CONCEPT
Jop van Bennekom
Helios Capdevila

PRODUCTION
Alice Burkle
Imogen Scott

PUBLISHER
Stefan McGrath

MARKETING DIRECTOR
Nicola Hill

BRAND MANAGER
Sam Voulters

PICTURE RESEARCH
Samantha Johnson

CONTRIBUTORS
Naomi Alderman, Travis Elborough, Reinier Gerritsen, Benjamin Alexander Huseby, Andreas Larsson, Yann Le Bec, Nicholas Lezard, Yelena Moskovich, Simon Price, Megan Wray Schertler, Lina Scheynius, Bruno Staub, Sadie Stein, Trey Taylor, Elin Unnes.

THANK YOU
Magnus Åkesson, Daniel Björk, Sarah Death, Lauren Elkin, David Foy, Jordan Kelly, Rebecca Lee, Penny Martin, Rebecca Morris, Annick Muller, Magnus Nilsson, Norvik Press, Caroline Pretty, Rosa Rankin-Gee, Rino Rotevatn, Luiza Sauma, Nichola Smalley, Saskia Vogel, Jeanette Ward, Sylvia Whitman.

Penguin Books
80 Strand
London WC2R 0RL

info@thehappyreader.com
www.thehappyreader.com

SNIPPETS

If books were birds then these are the songs they'd sing this spring.

EURO STAR — When a passenger on the train from London to Paris began reading a literary journal, the man sitting next to her remarked that the issue contained a beautiful review of Max Porter's novel *Grief is the Thing with Feathers*. Yes, she replied. As it happened, Porter's book was in her possession, and she was holding off from looking at the review until she finished reading it, in case she disagreed with it. The man then formally introduced himself: my name, he told her, is Max Porter.

*

CURRY — Monks at Downside Abbey in Somerset discovered a cookbook from 1793, with dishes including 'fricassee of pigs feet and ears', mockturtle soup (using calves' heads and feet instead of turtles), plus one of the earliest known English-language recipes for chicken curry.

*

FRACTAL FICTION — Scientists at the Institute of Nuclear Physics in Poland have found that James Joyce's novel *Finnegans Wake* is constructed exactly like the mathematical patterns known as 'multifractals'. Fractals are patterns that look similar no matter the scale at which they are observed; multifractals form when several fractals are interwoven. In a book this might mean that any given fragment has a structure that mirrors the entire work. The scientists also made similar claims about *The Waves* by Virginia Woolf and *Hopscotch* by Julio Cortázar.

*

LOVING IT — A pair of Los Angeles-based sisters have opened a bookshop dedicated exclusively to the romance genre. The Ripped Bodice, say Bea and Leah Koch, will combat the stigma attached to the romance genre, offering a 'physical space where romance enthusiasts can come together to buy the books they love'.

SNIPPETS

CLUB MIX — The meaning of the term 'book club' continues to warp and find new shapes. Emma Watson's feminist book club, Our Shared Shelf, plays out via discussion boards on the website Goodreads; Florence Welch's Between Two Books is a nomadic affair straddling Instagram, Twitter and Facebook; and Mark Zuckerberg's Year of Books, which concluded in December, took the form of — what else? — vast Facebook comment threads. Even the so-called dark web, where users browse anonymously for various, occasionally criminal, reasons, has covert clubs discussing titles of a revolutionary or left-field nature, and has also recently even gained its own literary magazine, *The Torist*.

*

ADAPT — The BBC has commissioned a television adaptation of *The Woman in White*, Wilkie Collins' proto-detective novel, and, long-standing readers will remember, the first ever *Happy Reader* Book of the Season.

*

PROGRESS — Across Britain, telephone boxes are being transformed into 'mini-libraries'. Whether complementing the village noticeboard in Wall, Staffordshire, or providing second-hand fiction to residents of Lewisham, South-East London, a spate of conversions is giving the iconic red structures, their original function now more or less redundant thanks to the total domination of mobile technology, a new life.

*

NEST — In 1827, a Leeds-based aristocrat named Lady Isabella Hertford had an excellent interior-design idea: plastering the walls of her Chinese drawing room with pictures from John James Audubon's illustrated book *Birds of America*. It has become the world's most expensive wallpaper: had the now incredibly rare tome been left intact it could have fetched around £7m at auction. Looks nice, though.

*

BOURGEOIS — Said a customer at the London Review Bookshop in Bloomsbury: 'I'm looking for *Bourgeois Utopias*.' Said a member of staff: 'This is one, isn't it?'

*

MARK — A British man who was fined £60 for dropping a bookmark was pleased when the fine was overturned. David Ellis had been reading comic cricket memoir *Penguins Stopped Play* outside the premises of rail manufacturers Faiveley Transport, Birkenhead. His claim not to have realised his bookmark had slipped was upheld by the county council.

*

EAT ME — A survey has found that the book most people have lied about reading is not, in fact, Leo Tolstoy's *War and Peace* or David Foster Wallace's *Infinite Jest* but Lewis Carroll's children's favourite (or not, as it turns out) *Alice's Adventure's in Wonderland*.

What is it with Ethan Hawke? Is he Hollywood's favourite indie actor or the indies' favourite Hollywood actor (or none of the above)? Flung into stardom from an early age, the Texas-born 45-year-old has spent a successful career maintaining a focus and integrity that put him in a category of approximately one. From the still-undimmed resonance of *Dead Poets Society* to staggeringly ambitious arthouse films such as *Boyhood* and the *Before* trilogy (both of whose long-running processes entailed that we actually watch Hawke age on screen) his work has involved an intensity that we might term, for want of a better word, 'novelistic'. Indeed, how many screen icons have written critically successful novels, or tried, as per his recent book *Rules for a Knight*, to set out serious moral philosophies? As we learn in this in-depth interview, his work has tended to find both grounding and inspiration in the world of books, with his reading habits roaming between subjects — from jazz pianos to baby raccoons — with wild abandon.

ETHAN HAWKE

ETHAN HAWKE
(06-11-70)

Born in: Austin, Texas. Lives in: Brooklyn, New York. Stage debut: school production of *Saint Joan* (aged 13). Screen debut: *Explorers* (aged 14). Films include: *Dead Poets Society* (1989), *Reality Bites* (1994), *Before Sunrise* (1995), *Training Day* (2001), *Boyhood* (2014). Novels: *The Hottest State* (1996), *Ash Wednesday* (2002). Moral handbook: *Rules for a Knight* (2015). Graphic novel: *Indeh: A Story of the Apache Wars* (2016, with Greg Ruth). Children: Maya (b. 1998), Levon (b. 2002), Clementine Jane (b. 2008), Indiana (b. 2011). Height: 1.79m. Islands owned: 1.

In conversation with
SADIE STEIN

Portraits by
BRUNO STAUB

ETHAN HAWKE

NEW YORK

I meet Ethan Hawke in a loft in Chinatown — our handy location for a sprawling conversation and a tasty lunch. For years the actor has lived in Brooklyn with his wife and children. Hawke is high energy and friendly, unfailing and generous in his enthusiasms — writing down titles that intrigue him, and talking books, music and movies with an unpretentious excitement. (He also compliments my moccasins.) The breadth of his consumption would be noteworthy for anyone — although he bemoans not having more time to read — but even by his own prolific standards, this has been a busy period.

An actor since the age of thirteen, Hawke has made more than sixty-five films. As I write, a new biopic of jazz trumpeter Chet Baker is about to hit theatres, a book for young people called *Rules for a Knight* is already on the shelves, and *Indeh*, a graphic novel about the Apache Wars (written with artist Greg Ruth) is in galleys. At forty-five, he has written two other novels and collaborated on screenplays (he was nominated for Oscars for two of the *Before* trilogy, as well as for his performance in *Training Day*), directed a documentary, plays and two feature films; and has already made three movies in 2016. And yet he exhibits no sense of being rushed or on a job — he gives the conversation his full, interested attention. Incidentally, he describes himself as unusually underemployed.

SADIE: I can't get over how intact your teeth are, after so recently seeing you as Chet Baker in *Born to be Blue*.

ETHAN: You know, one of the nicest things about playing that part, believe it or not, was my whole life I've had these really crooked teeth. And after Chet gets beat up and he gets the dentures put in, you know, I had to have those dentures made, and I so enjoyed being photographed with straight teeth. I was thinking, what is it that I like about this? Oh, my teeth aren't crooked.

S: I mean his dentures were impeccable. But not, I imagine, the primary allure of the part.

E: It's a fascinating part of his life's journey and it's weird how the universe conspires against people. You know, we all have weaknesses and strengths and Chet had this weakness: he was always worried about his embouchure. And then he lost a tooth as a kid and that got him. And *then* some dealer beats him up and he loses all his teeth and it's in this place that all his weakness is revealed. And it's also his greatest strength: the tenderness in his voice *and* the way he plays.

S: Did you read many biographies prior to starting?

E: I read pretty much all of the serious ones, and the not serious ones. I love his memoir, *As Though I Had Wings*. A lot of the most sensational biographies, they really loved to tell the story of the most debauched escapades. And the trouble with that, according to a bunch of his friends and people who cared about him, is that you're not really seeing the best Chet. Whenever you're studying a junkie who can't get their drugs, it's not a very appealing portrait, and he was a full-blown addict pretty much all his adult life. But there were a lot of wonderful stories.

S: Do you typically read a lot for your roles?

E: Yeah. But it's particularly necessary when you're playing a real person. There was a great jazz book called *But Beautiful* by Geoff Dyer, and I was really inspired by that book. And it gave me permission to realise that the truth of who Chet Baker is is relevant and important to the people who loved him, his family, and that no movie or book or article written about him is going to change the truth. And what Geoff Dyer did was kind of attack the legend, is try to go, why does Duke Ellington mean so much to me? And when I think of Duke Ellington what do I think of? And when I put on a jazz record what do I think of?

S: In some ways I know it wasn't an exact overlap, but working on that and then thinking about your book *Rules for a Knight*, which is essentially a moral guide, it must have been an interesting contrast.

E: Well, I've worked on *Rules for a Knight* for years. It's kind of this little project I gave myself, that started out a very literal ... what's the right word for it? Just a need-based project. We really wanted the kids to have certain rules in the house and we decided to come up with these seven rules that our household had — things like bedtime and dinner and homework. But they all sounded so banal to me that I started looking for a larger ethos: *why* you should eat well every day and *why* you should get a good night's sleep ... My wife and I started

1. EMBOUCHURE
—
If attempting to befriend a brass or woodwind musician then casually dropping in the term 'embouchure' — meaning 'the way in which a player applies their mouth to the mouthpiece, especially as it effects the production of sound' — is a fairly effective strategy.

THE HAPPY READER

riffing on *why* — what is important? So it just kept growing like a little book, like a snowball. I kept being inspired by or having an experience that would speak to *Rules*.

S: One of the things I really like about *Rules for a Knight* is the recommended reading list in the 'thank yous' in the back. It becomes a de facto — I won't say Great Books list — but a kind of self-taught philosophy course.

E: I mean, when life gets hard, it's hard to have a philosophy and particularly if you want to challenge yourself — and not to sign up for a pre-existing set of rules: I get baptised this day, I get confirmed this day, I do this. There's a rule book whether you're raised in the Jewish faith or you're raised as a Muslim or a Christian or whatever — you can sign up and kind of turn your brain off and just do what the priest tells you to do. But if you're uncomfortable with that, like I was as a young person, it's hard. So I challenged myself to give my kids a way to think about things without ever using the word 'God'. It wasn't that I didn't love aspects of religion or organised religion — there is nothing I enjoy reading about more than people seriously trying to figure out why we're born, why we have to die and why loved ones have to die. That fascinates me.

S: What were some of your philosophical inspirations?

E: You know, Philip Seymour Hoffman passed away while I was working on this. And River Phoenix and Phil are two of the major influences on my life as an actor — they're the first peers of mine that were really fully mature artists, where there's some kind of self-expression happening through their performances. River and Phil were heroes to me in that way — River particularly when I was young, obviously. I was friends with Phil. For the last decade or more, every time I did a play and I didn't want to do it — it was some Wednesday matinee, I was tired or something like that — I would trick myself into thinking, 'Today's the day Phil's coming.' It was a game I'd play with myself to get it up for whatever audience is out there.

S: It's like he's your Fat Lady.

E: Yeah. He was Seymour's Fat Lady. Who are you going to sing for? But it seemed more than that because it's somebody very specific who you could pitch yourself against, about whom you would think, 'Ah, I can't do that shitty job for the money, River would think I was such a phoney.' And both of them lost to heroin. So in a way that did speak to *Rules for a Knight*, because people think, if you talk about the idea of ethics or having an ethos, that you live by some kind of airy-fairy ideal — they put these kind of really insipid labels on it like

2. THANK YOUS
—
Hawke's acknowledgments in *Rules for a Knight* are entitled 'Special Thanks to Other Knights'. These include Victor Hugo, Mother Ann Lee and River Phoenix.

3. SEYMOUR'S FAT LADY
—
In J. D. Salinger's novel *Franny and Zooey*, the so-called 'Fat Lady' — an imaginary woman on a sunny porch who seems to have been dreamed up by their late older brother Seymour — acts as a stand-in for a religious deity. She's a figure worth pleasing, a reminder that spirituality is everywhere and of how it's important that 'every person, no matter how egotistical or stupid' — yes, even this lady — 'deserves their respect'.

4. SEYMOUR: AN INTRODUCTION

Hawke's 2014 documentary film, the last of this interview's three quickfire references to the name 'Seymour', documents the life and career of the classical pianist Seymour Bernstein, who quit his life as a concert pianist in order to be able to teach. The title is identical to that of a novella by J. D. Salinger.

5. TITANIC

James Cameron's 1997 blockbuster has for years been dogged by a debate about the 'don't let go!' scene in which a raft-borne Rose (played by Kate Winslet) releases the hand of her lover Jack (played by Leonardo DiCaprio), dooming him to a grim, icy ocean death. Many have claimed, and some might say convincingly proved, that there was room on the raft and she could have just dragged him on board. Now Kate Winslet has come out in favour of this theory, telling US chat show host Jimmy Kimmel: 'There was plenty of room on the raft.'

'self-help'. Because if you say 'self-help', it implies there's something corny or something cultish or guru-ish, a lack of intelligence, for some reason. But without a philosophy, without something you believe in, it's very hard to know why you shouldn't shoot up and disappear. Did you see the documentary I did called *Seymour: An Introduction*?

S: Yes.

E: Well, one of the things Seymour Bernstein talks about is that if success in the arts isn't linked to your development as a person, then it really doesn't matter. That you can have all the success in the world, but if it's not in the service of something greater than your personal agenda, it's going to throw your whole life out of balance. And I think one of the things that Chet didn't have is that: what was he doing it for besides his own legend? Because it gives you a reason to stay sober or not to ruin your life. There are the obvious things, like how much better a father he probably could have been, how much better a lover he could have been, or a husband or a friend. But how much more music he could have made...

S: I wonder if his beauty must have been crippling when he first came on the scene.

E: It's crippling. But at the same time, there are people... I once hung out with DiCaprio in a few of the days after *Titanic* came out, and I just watched the way people reacted to him. Every little bit of celebrity that I've had, he had it times ten. I know what it tastes, it feels like, that people treat you differently and all that. But he had it to an absolutely, to a drowning effect. When you see how much great art he's put into the world, he's channelled all that attention coming at him and he funnelled it into movies. And I really admire him for it. And you can tell he's in service of something bigger than the DiCaprio agenda... not only is he making great art, he's also helping to show other young actors what is possible. Did you see the Amy Winehouse doc, *Amy*? I was really moved by it, but if you look at Amy Winehouse versus looking at Seymour Bernstein, we live in a culture that loves watching people set themselves on fire and we're hypnotised by it, we love stopping at the car accident to watch it happen. It's much harder to figure out how to live.

S: And she never had a moment of living.

E: I know. And it's like, dammit, you know, it's hard. If we want to take River and Phil as an example, it's hard in your early twenties and it's hard in your early forties. Life doesn't stop. There are these transitions life keeps asking you to make. You're constantly being asked to grow up, and growing up also means letting go of things, and letting go of what worked for you in the past or letting go of anger that may be motivating, so it's confusing. And it's why I love writing and it's why I like acting.

S: I was wondering, have you read Alfred Hayes? He was a British screenwriter primarily, who wrote two novels, *In Love*, which is the New York one, and *My Face for the World to See*, which is the Hollywood one.

E: That's a great title.

S: They're fantastic I think. I hate people going on about small masterpieces all the time, because a lot of things are just small, or justly forgotten. But in this case it's great, they're hard-boiled but not excessively... They're short too.

E: I'll write that down and I'll text it to myself. I love it when people recommend a book that isn't too long! If life lets me do it, you know, I really want to write a really good novel about the theatre and I really want to write a really good novel about the movies. I had this very weird experience yesterday that I promise you, if I get to live long enough, will be the novel. I went to a film programme for kids and they were showing *Explorers*. At thirteen, I was on the JV football team in West Windsor in New Jersey, living the most average life that you can possibly have, and through a kid who lived down the street I heard about an open call for one of the biggest-budget movies of all time. It was thirty million dollars to make *Explorers*. It was the same director who did *Gremlins*. It was going to be huge. Every kid in the country could go in. And I got this part, and I found myself in it, and I went and saw it the other day and I realised, oh shit, this is the novel I've been supposed to write. You know, it was my *Huck Finn*. In a lot of ways young people absorb the worst and the best of the movie business. All those serpents and diseases of vanity are all right there at the first rung of the ladder. River Phoenix, Jason Presson and I were in it. I took my kids on this snowy afternoon. I brought the slate for everybody to see, and the kids there were so interested in how I got the part and what it was like to make it. And here was River, who died of a drug addiction at twenty-three and Amanda Peterson, who died of a drug addiction at forty-three or whatever. Jason doesn't act any more. And it was like being tossed into a ring of fire. And it seemed so wonderful and yet it's like a dance with a tiger or something, and most people don't survive it. And I somehow survived this experience. And I could fictionalise it in a really interesting way.

S: I hope you will.

E: All of a sudden I realise that my experience in *Dead Poets*

6. JV FOOTBALL TEAM IN WEST WINDSOR
—
Junior varsity, or 'JV', football players are members of a high school football team who are a level below the main players in a competition, usually due to age. Based on scholing, Hawke would have played for the West Windsor-Plainsboro High School South Pirates.

7. HUCK FINN
—
Earlier this year, having just read Mark Twain's Mississippi-set *The Adventures of Huckleberry Finn*, three schoolchildren in Uttar Pradesh, India, made headlines when they decided to run away on their own Twain-inspired odyssey. Having travelled — in school uniform — by van, car and auto-rickshaw to the nearby city of Agra, they were eventually detained by railway officials.

Society, *White Fang* and *Explorers* could turn into one very interesting novel. Because I can see it from so many points of view, now. I don't want to write a memoir about *Explorers*, but if I could really write a serious novel... But anyway, the point being, you told me that this guy wrote his New York book and his LA book, so I want a New York and an LA book.

S: I don't why but I feel sure you'll like him. So who do you love? What books do you love?

E: Have you read *Limonov*? I'm reading it now. I've just read James McBride's *The Good Lord Bird*, which I just kind of went apeshit over. Have you read that? Isn't his voice incredible? I think one of the things I've been learning most recently is how important it is to keep your wit. Whenever an artist loses their wit, they end up taking themselves too seriously or they think their work is important. McBride couldn't be writing about a more serious subject, the abolitionist John Brown, and yet it's laugh-out-loud funny, without making a joke of the situation. I ended up being more rocked by that, by the pure humanity of it, because you end up loving the black characters *and* you love the white characters, too, because you see the humanity in it all, you see where everybody's coming from. And that book had the most Mark Twain in it of anything I've read for a while. Did you read Williams' *Stoner*? I think for me *Stoner* is the middle-aged *Catcher in the Rye*.

S: I just read about his other book about the kid who goes out West to hunt buffalo.

E: Oh my God. The buffalo one. What's it called? I mean I literally put that book down and I told my wife, 'I think it's one of the best books I ever read.' She said, 'Should I read it?' And I said, 'No. It's too horrible.' I know you're not allowed to say anything bad about Cormac McCarthy, but sometimes Cormac McCarthy is so macho and he's just so unsparing and unflinching and all those words everybody loves that I just find him, like, gruelling. Whereas... what the hell was the name of that book? John Williams... It's a much better title than *Stoner*, for Christ's sake. He has another book, *Augustus*. But we're going to remember in two seconds. See, I was working on the graphic novel *Indeh* when I read the buffalo book. And the genius of, if we could remember the name of this book, it shows what we did to the buffalo is what we did to the whales, which is what we're doing to the whole planet. We just don't stop throttling something until it's absolutely gone. And I don't know that I would ever want to see a movie of that book. I'm going to look it up. I now can't think of anything else except...

---

8. LIMONOV
—
French author Emmanuel Carrère's 2011 book *Limonov* is tricky to categorise, and tends to be described using terms like 'biographical novel' or even 'knowingly inaccurate biography'. Its subject is Eduard Limonov, the Russian writer and occasional dissident who rose to prominence during the Soviet era via an odd combination of poetry and hooliganism. Limonov has since written novels, launched a newspaper, founded a political party, and, in 2001, spent time in prison for (allegedly) attempting to raise a personal army with which to invade Kazakhstan.

S: I was wondering if you'd read the nameless buffalo book when I read *Indeh*.

E: Yeah. John Williams... Let's see if we can get it. I really want it to come to me, I'd just like my brain to function. *Butcher's Crossing*! I know what I was going to say. Isn't it so much like *The Revenant*? *The Revenant* is clearly inspired by *Butcher's Crossing*, don't you think? In a way I would say *Butcher's Crossing* is more about the greed of mankind, the blood of the oil industry.

S: It's not just purposeless agony. Have you ever read Buffalo Bill's memoirs?

E: Never.

S: I won't say a *good* book, but fascinating.

E: Have you read Calamity Jane's letters to her daughter?

S: No! I will now!

E: It's totally awesome, you have to read it. One of the best books I read this year is Jeff Lemire's graphic novel *Essex County* — it's so touching and it's different from a novel. I'd be really surprised if you sit down and look at that, spend an afternoon with it, and you're not really moved. You'll remember it like you remember reading *Franny and Zooey* or something — it gets to you. Some people like Greg, my co-author on *Indeh*, grew up on comics — I didn't — and he understands the language: it was really through this process that I learned a lot about it and I grew to love it. He taught me, 'Look: the thing is that when reading a good graphic novelist, you need to study the picture. This indicates flashback, this indicates something else...' There's a way that a lot of thirteen-year-old boys stare at the picture. 'How's this gun in the holster? Who's saying that? What's the difference between that guy and that guy?' There are lots of clues inside each frame. In a good graphic novel the frame is full of little paintings, and when something is given a double space it doesn't mean, 'Oh, they just liked this drawing better' — it means it's to be studied more, whereas little cursory close-ups of eyes and things like that have their own little tale.

S: How do you have time to read as much as you do?

E: I don't. It's awful. And also that my life as an actor requires me to read screenplays, which is a little like, if you're a chef, having to be a taster for a candy maker. I get a lot of scripts. I've been doing it since I was thirteen. I've read a lot of screenplays. But that's the hardest thing about my life — I mean, not the hardest thing about my life, that's just so pathetic, that's how great my life is — but what I mean is,

9. CALAMITY JANE

How exactly did the frontierswoman and performer Martha Jane Cannary come to be known as Calamity Jane? It depends who you ask. Jane claimed the nickname was given to her by an army captain who she'd saved from a calamitous situation involving a bullet and a horse. Others said that this story was invented, and the name sprung up because Jane was in the habit of warning others that to mess with her was to 'court calamity'.

10. TASTER FOR A CANDY MAKER

Swizzels, the brand behind Lovehearts, did in fact recently advertise for the position of 'official taster'. Michelle Eland, a 40-year-old teaching assistant, triumphed against more than 2,500 rival applicants.

THE HAPPY READER

Literary passion runs in the family: Hawke's great-granduncle was the *Cat on a Hot Tin Roof* playwright Tennessee Williams. Photography assistance: Andrew Beardsworth. Grooming: Lisa-Raquel.

ETHAN HAWKE

11. MILES

—

The long-anticipated Miles Davis biopic, *Miles Ahead*, is now screening in cinemas, starring Don Cheadle as Davis, and Ewan McGregor as a *Rolling Stone* journalist determined, despite an early punch in the face, to write a profile of the fabled jazz trumpeter and bandleader. Cheadle directed and co-wrote the movie, and even learned to play the trumpet.

one of the things I like least about being an adult is that I used to get to read so much. I travel a lot and I read a lot on planes, but that's really not the same. If I'm doing a movie about Chet Baker, 'OK, what's my job now?' Well, I've got to read that Art Pepper book, I've got to read the Hampton Hawes book. And obviously I have to read all the Chet Baker biographies and then you've got to read the book about Miles because you've got to know, OK, well if you read the book about Miles you've got to read the... You know. And so there's this one year of my life where I read all this jazz non-fiction. And you do a Cormac McCarthy movie and you read about Cormac McCarthy. And you do this, that and the other thing, and you do a Tom Stoppard play and... And so my life is full of chapters where it's my job to read. But I have huge holes... I didn't graduate from college, I don't have a proper education. I have a friend who likes to say 'You got your education from hearsay university' — you know, it's just like I've been bullshitting in diners and bars for going on thirty years.

S: Well, you do that at college.

E: Yeah, well, I kind of did that my whole life! I remember being at a screening of Richard Linklater's *Waking Life*, a movie I loved, and I walked out and some guy said, 'That movie was the worst!' and I said, 'Why?' He says, 'Whoever made this movie never left college,' and while I beg to differ, I know what he means — he means that this whole movie's like staying up all night at college — and I'm like, why would you ever stop doing that? Those are the greatest nights of my life, so why grow up and turn your brain off or something? A large portion of my education as it were comes from making a Western and somebody going, 'Have you read...?' Some stunt guy says, 'Have you read Calamity Jane's letters? She used to go out with Wild Bill Hickok, you've got to read these letters!' They're amazing, I'm not even sure if they're real, they're so good. But I also love getting recommendations from people, because we all live in our little sphere and you stick to the same kind of friends and they give you the same kind of books and you listen to the same kind of albums. I'm always kind of horrified when I think I've discovered some piece of music in some really weird way and I play it for a friend and they know all the words and I hadn't seen them in two years. It just makes you realise.

S: But I imagine you meet a lot of people — and a wide range of people — which for something like music is great, because at a certain point most of us realise we've stopped having the energy to follow it, and we get in ruts.

E: I know, it is really cool because my life is constantly changing, I'm always in different settings and it makes it really easy to remember your life. My dad sometimes will say, 'Well, what year was that?', and why would you remember the difference between '98 and '94 when you had exactly the same job, you're with the same people, you live in the same house. All that changed is the small people were different sizes, whereas for me, I remember ... 'So where were you in 2014?' 'Oh, I was shooting the Chet Baker movie.' 'I was in LA — that was the year *Boyhood* came out.' It's always changing — I like that about my life.

S: Did your parents read when you were growing up?

E: Voraciously. I'll never read as much as they do. A lot of my favourite books have come to me via my father, and not even just from a young age. Just yesterday or two days ago or whatever, Greg Ruth, my co-author on *Indeh*, and I got a quote from Joseph Boyden, who is one of my favourite authors. He wrote *Three Day Road* and *Through Black Spruce*, and he's great. The fact that he likes our book means so much, and I wouldn't know who Joseph Boyden is if it wasn't for my dad. My dad writes to me, 'You've got to read this,' because he just eats up literature. He is an equal opportunity reader. He reads Tom Clancy and he reads those books about the — oh, everybody loves them but — the *Master and Commander* books? I can't remember that guy's name.

S: Patrick O'Brian, yeah.

E: Yes, and he reads everything; he'll read Kurt Vonnegut and he'll read Flannery O'Connor. One thing I really admire is when people as they age are still doing things for fun. The way that you felt reading a comic book when you were fourteen, if that's what you enjoyed — there's literature out there that you'll enjoy reading that much. There are movies that you'll want to see that will make you feel like a kid again. You just have to make sure you're not going to see that movie just because it won the Oscar or somebody in your office told you it was good. You've got to chase your own nose. Rock and roll is the easiest, when you discover something you love — because you can't fake it. You don't like a song because someone told you to like it, because we're all sometimes horrified by what song we secretly love, right? I have a seventeen-year-old now and seventeen-year-olds are cool, so my seventeen-year-old turned me on to an album the other day and I'm like, 'This is the best music I've heard in ages!' and what's the guy's name? Father John Misty. A great way to have your ear to the ground is to pay attention to your kids.

S: It's the best. Do they take recommendations from you?

E: My daughter has recently turned the corner and has now

12. FATHER JOHN MISTY
—
Topically enough, the singer Father John Misty is touring the US and Europe this spring, beginning in Santa Ana, California on 30 March and concluding in Oslo, Norway, on 31 May.

13. HAMILTON

The smash Broadway show is currently sold out until well into 2017 — and is a wonderful example of what might happen following a random book purchase. Lin-Manuel Miranda had the unlikely idea (for a hip-hop musical about US founding father Alexander Hamilton) while reading Ron Chernow's 800-page biography, which he had bought on impulse to read while on holiday.

decided that she'll ask me. The other day she started this little film society with her friends and they were like, 'We're going to start a film society, what shall we watch?' and I was like, 'Have you seen *Five Easy Pieces*?' 'No' and they watched it and they loved it and I was so proud. They really got it. They had all these interesting things to say about it, and so she's listening to me, and I haven't let her down, I turned her on to some cool stuff. I took her to see *Hamilton* — her eyes popped out in that show. Did you ever go on YouTube and see Lin-Manuel Miranda's performance for Obama when he was first coming up with this idea?

S: No.

E: Oh, you've got to watch it and treat yourself, it's Miranda at some benefit or something and it's just him playing all the parts and he's clearly writing it. It's very different, but he's just plugged into something vital.

S: He seems to be a really nice, good guy too.

E: My daughter showed me him on the Jimmy Fallon show and he's literally like a friend of yours in high school or something. He's so excited to be on the show, and he's so damn earnest he's impossible not to like. There's a great Lily Allen quote about becoming famous which is like, 'I feel like I'm running for office,' because there's all this accountability and everybody wants you to be nice to them. That sounds easy except when you're trying to walk your kid to school and fourteen people want you to be nice to them and then they're actively hurt if you go about your day. And then they stumble on you when your dog died and they feel as if you don't have any other life, you know? You just have to put on this fake face all the time and it's exhausting and it cuts you off at the heels a little bit.

S: One thing I was thinking, it must make it harder to fight and argue about things like books.

E: Well, it does, because even as I'm talking to you I have to worry about, 'Okay, well, who's going to be...?' You never want to disparage anybody. But it's fun to have a goddamn opinion. So if you say that *The Revenant* isn't perfect, well then all of a sudden you'll never work for anybody that made *The Revenant* again. But that's what homogenises the dialogue outside and it's so exhausting to hear everybody just say milk about everything.

S: I think the main utility, at least in my life, of school is a safe space for fighting. I mean the classroom, not the dorm room.

E: I'm talking about this a lot because my daughter is applying to college and she's going, 'Should I go to college?' and I just think it's so important to give yourself a place to disappear a little bit and form your opinions and your identity and have a place to fight it out and a place that's not... So much of what happened to me is — I had to do a lot of my learning in public, so there's this accountability... I mean, thank God you haven't mentioned Jack Kerouac. I did some interviews when *Reality Bites* came out, and I had just read the Jack Kerouac canon and I talked about it a lot. Well, a lot of 25-year-olds are really into Jack Kerouac and I still support that and think he speaks to a part of an aspect of — particularly young men. However, I'm done talking about it. *Catcher in the Rye* right now is a book for me to give to my son. I had to do all that in public and you have to learn who you are and make all these mistakes — and I see the value, particularly if you want to be an artist, of writing some really bad short stories and getting told they're bad or doing a really fucked-up version of an Ionesco play where everybody is wearing blood or something like that. I saw *Tootsie* the other day [*both laugh*] and one of my favourite moments in that movie is when the guys says something like, 'I don't want a packed house on Broadway, I want a ninety-seat house in a theatre that only plays when it rains, and I don't want somebody coming to me after the show and saying "Good job!" I want somebody coming to me two weeks later and saying, "What the hell was that?"' You remember that line? I'm paraphrasing wildly, but that's the gist: you need to have that space, and then you need to figure out who you are and then go out and do it.

S: Lena Dunham was always so poised in that regard.
　　E: Absolutely, it makes me believe in reincarnation of some sort.

S: I didn't think she got sufficient credit for that — at that age.
　　E: This woman arrived on the planet Earth with a mission. Several of my favourite young women, really serious actors, worked with her and came back feeling inspired and challenged. Nobody gave her that and nobody gave her the voice and nobody gave her the content, or the originality for that matter. She's actually one of those artists that even if you don't like her, I really value what she's doing by giving people the voice to speak against what she's doing. You know? That's really the job of the artist. There's a great Ginsberg quote where the job of the artist is not to be liked or win prizes or win fans; the job of the artist is to provoke conversation and to penetrate. He'd gone on the *Carson Show* dressed as a Hare Krishna and he said, 'You think I don't know people think I'm nuts? But I don't want some kind of guy — I want some guy in Mid America to wake up at 3am in his little suburban house going, "What the hell did that guy say?"'

S: It would be nice if we got more of that now or it wasn't just 'Oh, someone's off the wagon', which is the only time in which we see anyone behaving with any variation — you don't have eccentricity, you have erratic behaviour.

E: It's interesting, isn't it? It's hard to be eccentric in public because you just get beaten up so badly. It's amazing, us going through the whole machine of the Oscars last year with *Boyhood* and watching Ellar Coltrane and Lorelei Linklater and wanting to protect them through all that. Ellar is so fun. He wanted to go to the Oscars in a dress, but at the same time the whole corporation of people that invested so much money in us being there and getting there, you feel you're part of a bigger machine than yourself. You feel responsibility to that and it just homogenises everything, and it's so hard. And you watch what it does to young women. It's brutal, watching Lorelei — people blog about what she wears, and knowing her friends are reading it and she's a young person... Is that our lunch? Thanks!

LUNCH TIME

We've ordered lunch from a nearby Thai restaurant — large bowls of spicy, noodle-thick soup, perfect for the cold, snowy day. Hawke comments on the excellence of the music playing in the background; an infectious mix of Sam Cooke, reggae deep-cuts, indie rock. 'There hasn't been a bad one!' he remarks happily.

S: If you say Philip Seymour Hoffman was your motivator when you went on stage, do you have someone like that for your writing? A dream reader?

E: I got to do Tom Stoppard's *The Coast of Utopia*, which is three plays — basically eight hours, nine hours, about mid-nineteenth-century Russian revolutionaries. The most interesting thing about that whole process was being in a rehearsal room with Tom Stoppard for that long. The attention to detail, the care and passion and artistry that he puts into forming a sentence; I didn't know human beings thought that way. You see it sometimes in sports: the way a guy will work on his serve, the way Peyton Manning will practise throwing the football every day, not just some days, but every day. Well, that's the way Tom Stoppard views a comma. I remember he came up to

ETHAN HAWKE

As Mason's dad in *Boyhood* (2014).

A comma can mean the difference between laughter and silence (see p. 26).

With Philip Seymour Hoffman in *Before the Devil Knows You're Dead* (2007).

An American buffalo (see p. 16).

With River Phoenix and Jason Presson in *Explorers* (1985).

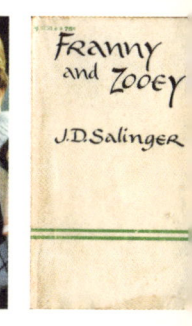

J. D. Salinger's novel *Franny and Zooey* (see p. 13).

Insignia of Hawke's high school football team (see p. 15).

As Chet Baker in *Born to Be Blue* (2015).

As Jack in *White Fang* (1991).

With Denzel Washington in *Training Day* (2001).

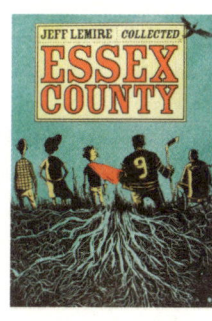

Jeff Lemire's graphic novel *Essex County* (see p. 17).

With Josh Charles, Robert Sean Leonard, Robin Williams and others in *Dead Poets Society* (1989).

me after a preview once and he said, 'Act one, scene three, your last line: is it "Well — comma — that won't do"? Or is it "Well that won't do" — no comma?' And I said, 'I don't know. I'll go look it up.' And I looked it up and came back and said, 'See, Tom, it's well — comma — that won't do.' And he said, 'Yes. I know.' His point being, I was reading it without a comma. And you might think, 'Oh my God, what is he talking about?' But the next night I do it with a comma and I get a huge laugh. The whole rhythm was different. I would watch him hand-write an idea for a speech, and then watch it get typed up, and then watch it get moved around, and watch the words get reversed, and watch him move that over there, and see how the whole mechanism worked. You leave with a buzz, like *I want that*. It's the same as watching anything done at a really high level. Every now and then in acting it happens — Jack Nicholson in *One Flew Over the Cuckoo's Nest* or something — where somebody sets the bar. I don't know if you saw Mark Rylance in *Jerusalem*? First of all the writing is electric and Jez Butterworth is an amazing playwright and the words are amazing. But you're watching an actor whose *life* has been the hard work of the performing arts, and here it was manifested. It was like watching Matisse in his room or something. I remember hearing Sean Penn say that about a Daniel Day-Lewis performance. He said, 'There are lots of performances I remember, but I always know how they did it, but every now and then with Daniel Day-Lewis I'm not sure how the hell he did that.'

S: Do you love not knowing?

E: I love it. It makes you a kid again. It was like that watching the way Stoppard played with words, and the way he loved to read and how much he's read. It would be so fun when you'd run into something he hadn't read. You know, I remember once mentioning Emerson's 'Divinity School Address'. And it was very funny because the British don't take the American philosophers that seriously. 'I haven't really looked at the transcendentalists. Perhaps I should.' I was like, 'You should, they're great. Promise.' 'Well, the Americans, they might have something to offer.' So, he, in a way, is my dream reader, ever since that experience.

S: Well, that's a good one.

E: Yeah. Because it makes you be super-discerning about your sentences. *Is that really what I mean?* It's fun, somebody who has such wit — to be that funny and that intelligent. A lot of intelligent people aren't very funny, somehow all the learning just kind of makes them very serious. But to have somebody that funny and that playful and that learned, it's really fun.

S: So you must have been totally immersed in the Apache Wars?

E: Yes.

S: Which is also a project a long time in the works, right?

E: It's a strange time. For twelve years I worked on *Boyhood*, that's over. I had this long *Before* trilogy, and that's over. I mean doing a graphic novel — you just wouldn't believe how long it takes. You can read them in twenty minutes and that's what's frustrating about it; at least if you write a novel it takes people a long time to read. But the graphic novel, people read it in half an hour, it doesn't change the fact you've got to work your ass on that for ages... and so that's coming to an end. *Rules for a Knight* is something I've been working on for a long time. I'm unemployed for the first time in a long time. For a few years I really threw myself back into my acting career, and I've made a lot more movies than I have in a while, than I did when I was younger... and my dog just died. I had this dog forever, I loved this animal and it really does feel like there's some new chapter about to happen and I'm not sure what it is.

S: I'm sorry. Did you have to have her put down?

E: No! This dog was like the most wonderful... entity, being, whatever you call them, in our house. She was so patient and loving and she never faked affection. She was funny and I just loved this animal and then — she was never any trouble, she was a Border Collie so they're really smart. I never needed a leash — the only time I ever put a leash on her was to make other strangers more comfortable. I'd walk my kids to school, she'd just sit at the front of the school and wait for us to come out. I'm telling you, from twelve years ago, when I took my eldest to kindergarten to this year when I was taking my youngest to kindergarten, she'd walk us — she'd sit out front and wait for us, and then one day she went in our backyard and started digging a hole under the porch. She didn't want to go for a walk or anything, and I carried her to the truck and took her to the vet, and it turned out she had a tumour on one of her glands, but she was going to be fine. But it burst and she had a heart attack and died. Just like that. And truth be known, she was old for a Border Collie. But she didn't seem like an elderly animal. Anyway I loved this dog.

S: What was her name?

E: Her name was Nina — I bought her on the same day that Nina Simone died.

S: What a privilege to have her in your life.

E: That's the way I have to start looking at it. I actually felt

14. BEFORE TRILOGY
—
Richard Linklater's trilogy about modern romance is structured around long, naturalistic conversations between its two leads, Jesse (Ethan Hawke) and Celine (Julie Delpy). In the second movie, *Before Sunset*, Jesse, an author, gives a reading from a novel at the famous Parisian bookshop, Shakespeare & Company. This January, Hawke visited the same bookshop to give a real reading from *Rules for a Knight*. 'I do think it's weird,' he told the crowd. 'I've shot a movie in here where I was pretending to do a book reading.'

15. DAY THAT NINA SIMONE DIED
—
Jazz singer Nina Simone died on 21 April 2003 in Carry-le-Rouet, France; Mark Twain also died on this date, in 1910.

16. SAY TO HER
—
Border Collies are known for their outstanding word comprehension. Indeed, the largest tested memory of any non-human belongs to Chaser, a Border Collie belonging to a retired psychologist in South Carolina. Chaser knows more than 1,000 words including the names of 800 cloth animals, 116 balls and 100 plastic toys, and can understand basic grammar.

that way the whole time I had her. I mean, she was like a movie dog. Literally, you could say to her 'Go and wake up Maya' and she'd run into Maya's room, or you could even play hide and seek with her. Invariably she would never let you hide because it was easy for her to find you.

S: No but it's... that's huge, losing...

E: Yeah, it was huge. It just happened a few days ago. I've always been a real sucker for animals. When I was young, I really hated going to church. My family is really religious: my stepfather was really serious about his faith, and my mum really had a more laissez-faire attitude, but she loves the choir. My stepfather said to me that I didn't have to go to church if I would do something for somebody else on Sunday mornings. He didn't want me to sit at home and just sleep in and watch football. What would I do? I needed to volunteer. And so I got a job working at the local ASPCA, and every Sunday morning I would go and walk the dogs and clean their cages and I did it for a couple of years and I absolutely loved it. But so many of these dogs would be put to sleep and you'd get to know them pretty well and — the older ones of course would never get adopted, and it's really hard. Then a couple of years after high school was over and I had started professional acting, I was offered Jack London's *White Fang*. I loved it, and I really loved *Call of the Wild* — people think it's kind of a children's book, but if you read it, it's mind-blowingly well written. I mean it's so beautiful.

S: Jack London is fantastic. *White Fang* is great; *The Sea-Wolf* is fantastic.

E: *The Sea-Wolf* is! Have you read *Martin Eden*? You know you're in trouble when you start obsessively reading the last five pages of *Martin Eden* again and again. I remember one period of my life where, with every friend that came over, it was like, 'Is this not the greatest thing?' and they start going, 'Dude, are you all right?' and actually I wasn't all right, but anyway the point being — I got to go out to Alaska and, this is no joke, I learned more about acting from the experience of working with these wolves on that movie. I had to work with these half wolfs and quarter wolfs. There was this animal trainer, a very magical person. You can't act with an animal, you actually have to be with them, which is the fundamental lesson: when you're onstage playing Macbeth you can't act like Macbeth, you've got to be Macbeth. And as soon as the animal senses you're worried about the camera, they look at the camera. They don't know to pretend — they can sense something fake about you and you have to just actually be with them. That's why so many of the old cowboy actors are so good

— they're actually worried about riding their horse and it makes them very present tense. But anyway the point is that I've always loved those kind of books — you remember the Sterling North book *Rascal* about a racoon, or *Sounder*? I've been a sucker for animal fiction my whole life. So *White Fang* was perfect for me. I've got to figure out my novel about the making of a movie — that probably has to do with animals somehow.

S: I love this idea.

    E: Do you think?

S: Yes.

SADIE STEIN is a freelance writer and a contributing editor to *The Paris Review*. She lives in New York, and is currently reading the letters that Calamity Jane wrote to her daughter.

THE HAPPY READER

Hawke just so happens to be reading this issue's Book of the Season (see p33 onwards).

SPRING READS

Fresh from Ethan's enormous bookshelves, a reading list to enhance the most zesty time of year.

GO TELL IT ON THE MOUNTAIN (1953)
James Baldwin

Not to be confused with the Christmas carol of the same name, James Baldwin's semi-autobiographical novel unfolds in 1930s Harlem. An astute teenager, John Grimes, is destined to follow in the footsteps of his father and become a preacher. He has doubts about his beliefs, a low-key hatred for his father, and a confusing crush on an older boy in the congregation. Baldwin's first novel did much to help assert his voice as one of the essential chroniclers of the Black American experience.

CITY OF THIEVES (2008)
David Benioff

In desperate need of a carton of eggs, two young men in World War II-era Leningrad tear through the city in order to fulfill a secret mission given them by a Soviet NKVD officer. The officer needs the eggs within five days to make his daughter's wedding cake, but this proves no mean feat. Eggs are a rare commodity and haven't been seen in Leningrad for months. The premise of this coming-of-age tale may come across as bizarre, but it's a thrilling account of a friendship formed under the most scrambled of circumstances.

CITY ON FIRE (2015)
Garth Risk Hallberg

The hive mind was collectively stumped when Hallberg, an unknown, unpublished author, emerged a literary superstar with a $2 million book deal – likely the highest advance for a debut novel ever. His 927-page tome is an ambitious dive into '70s New York. Tied together by a seemingly random shooting in Central Park, a handful of New Yorkers from different walks of life try to untangle the threads of their involvement. In keeping with spectacle, *The Girl with the Dragon Tattoo* producer Scott Rudin has already snapped up rights to adapt the story for the big screen.

A BRIEF HISTORY OF SEVEN KILLINGS (2014)
Marlon James

This lyrically beguiling novel reimagines the 1976 assassination attempt of Bob Marley in which, on the eve of the Jamaican general election, gunmen entered Marley's house to take his life. While a challenging read, it's been proffered by some critics as a candidate for required reading and won the Man Booker prize for fiction in 2015. Although the names and places of those involved in this historical account have been changed, it maintains a compelling urgency around an event concerning the leading figure of Jamaica's reggae scene.

THE GOOD LORD BIRD (2013)
James McBride

Henry Shackleford is a young slave living in Kansas Territory in 1857. It's a turbulent time as a war wages between pro-slavers and those who oppose it. When legendary abolitionist John Brown arrives in town, he gets into a violent argument with Henry's master and the pair are forced to leave town. Brown is under the assumption that Henry is a girl, so Henry must conceal his true identity and play along with the horrifying nickname he is given: 'Little Onion'. This moving portrait is on par with McBride's memoir published in 1995, *The Color of Water: A Black Man's Tribute to His White Mother.*

A PRAYER JOURNAL (2013)
Flannery O'Connor

O'Connor's slender (40-page) volume is described simply and accurately as a prayer journal. Written in private in the 1940s and long thought hidden, it was discovered by her former lover William A. Sessions and published 30 years after her death. The book is halved to include facsimiles of the entire journal in O'Connor's own hand. Twenty-one at the time of writing, it explores a young woman's relationship with the divine through each entry, as she grapples with a responsibility to be a vessel for God while doling out constant pleas to have her writing accepted.

BLACK LAMB AND GREY FALCON (1941)
Rebecca West

Famed for her coverage of The Nuremburg Trials in *The New Yorker*, West turned her sharp skills of observation to plenty of subjects throughout her esteemed career. This, perhaps her most celebrated work of fiction, is the result of a six week trip to Yugoslavia in 1937. In it, the author examines the history, people and politics of Yugoslavia. West's objective was 'to show the past side by side with the present it created.'

THE HAPPY
READER

Folk-tales, revelry and card games amid the forests and lakes of western Scandinavia: part two of The Happy Reader channels THE SAGA OF GÖSTA BERLING, the legendary novel by Selma Lagerlöf.

Bookish Quarterly — Issue n° 6

OPENING LINE

'At long last, the minister stood in the pulpit.' This line from Lagerlöf's novel is often described as one of the most famous opening lines in Swedish literature, but why? Scholars say it is a remarkably clever version of the classic 'once upon a time', both telling us that this minister is not entirely reliable and placing the author in a position of divine power.

INTRODUCTION

Nowhere is spring more meaningful than in a country with a devastating winter. It's a transformation evoked with dreamlike beauty among the many stories that constitute Selma Lagerlöf's 1891 classic *The Saga of Gösta Berling* — a novel, writes SEB EMINA, that is, and always has been, like nothing else out there.

DEEPLY SWEDISH

Selma Lagerlöf's 1891 novel *The Saga of Gösta Berling* gives the impression of not having been written but transcribed. An intrepid shorthand expert, it seems, has travelled across Sweden to pay a visit to a famed storyteller, in an ornate wooden rocking chair by some perfect cliché of a fireside. Then, above the crackle of flames and the fathomless call of the forest, her voice recalls a series of tales taking place in a community by a lake called Löven — in the Swedish province of Värmland — during the span of four seasons. Most of them feature a handsome, flawed and somewhat inconsistently drawn figure named Gösta (pronounced 'yoo-stuh') Berling. He starts proceedings as a minister, is quickly forced to quit, then washes up in an old ironworks, where he coexists with a band of what our narrator calls 'cavaliers' (a local term that means something along the lines of 'elderly adventuring reveller').

The narrator — we may as well call her 'Selma' — seems to have told these stories quite often. Not one to let veracity get in the way of drama, she is changing small details to suit the mood of this particular telling. Sometimes she wonders about the way the stories came to her, interrupting herself, muttering how a particular yarn may not have happened in the way she just told it. 'Who can know?' she asks, exasperated but with a mischievous smile. 'It was such a long time ago!'

Each chapter of *The Saga of Gösta Berling* belongs to a wider whole, and each is also a standalone tale. Many involve Berling's romantic entanglements, including a rip-roaring scene where he and a love interest are pursued through the night by a pack of wolves. Others have little to do with him: a hunter forges a silver bullet to kill a legendary bear; a cavalier leaves the cavaliers' ironworks on the back of a bull saying he is returning home to die. Each poses a question, then offers an unexpected answer. More than once, the reader will need to put the book down, look out of the window and try to puzzle out what it all means, both to the people in the story and the eternal question of, as Selma puts it, 'how a man could be both happy and good.'

Behind Selma the narrator is Selma Lagerlöf the author. When the novel — Lagerlöf's first — was released, many critics didn't care to distinguish between the two. Here is a naive voice, was the consensus, and that's exactly what gives the novel its curious power. So authentic! This assumption partly rested on the book's provenance. *The Saga of Gösta Berling* came into the world as an entry to a novel-writing competition arranged by a 'practical weekly magazine for women and the home.' Nobody expected this 32-year-old school teacher from Värmland to go on to win the Nobel Prize in Literature — the first woman to do so — or to become one of Sweden's pre-eminent literary giants, with a body of work that would still hold up in the twenty-first century. But so it was: mention her children's classic *The Wonderful Adventure of Nils* to anyone who grew up in a Nordic country and their eyes will mist over as they remember the sound of a parent's voice tracing a boy's intrepid journeys across Sweden on the back of a goose.

And yes, in *The Saga of Gösta Berling*, Lagerlöf knew exactly what she was doing. She knew there was a primal atmosphere to the old fairy tales she grew up with that could not be replicated with the machine-like realism fashionable elsewhere. She wanted the effect of reading the novel to be reminiscent of the first time we encounter 'Little Red Riding Hood' or 'Jack and the Beanstalk', the way it feels strangely like we know the surreal rhythm of these prehistoric stories already (perhaps we do: certain fairy tales are more or less scorched into our DNA).

For a contemporary reader, *The Saga of Gösta Berling* is not always an easy read. Characters are introduced and then ignored; quests are set up and then soon forgotten. And what exactly are we meant to feel about Gösta? One chapter he's a drunk, the next a lothario. He's a hero, a wise man, a waste of space. The novel has the logic of a dream. Or no, not a dream, a string of old stories told next to a time-worn fireside by an unreliable storyteller. Does she really not remember what happened earlier — as she sometimes feigns — or what is meant to happen next? Or is she just playing games? The truth, we come to realise, is that it doesn't really matter, as long as the story works according to its own rules, which it always seems to.

NATURE

Over the centuries, the Swedish wilderness has been somewhat tamed: where the wild things once were, they tend to not be any more. But in recent decades something unexpected happened — the wolves came back. And our subconscious, writes ELIN UNNES, is only too familiar with their howl.

A KILLER COMEBACK

Norrland — the northern region of Sweden, where kids learn how to forge their own knives in kindergarten, where the pine trees are an unchanging dark green all year round, and where white lichens form mats so thick that the ground looks covered in snowdrift even under a blazing summer sun — is where the wolves reappeared.

Back in the 1200s wolf hunts by farmers were not just encouraged but mandatory, and there were dire fines for anyone who missed a *battue*; later the punishment was replaced by a cash reward. During the 1800s, as gun quality improved, the hunts became more efficient. Between 1827 and 1839, 6,790 wolves were killed in Sweden. The packs moved further and further north, and by the time the wolf came under legal protection in 1966 it was estimated that approximately ten individuals were left. There were no packs though. No families meant no new wolves, and for several years still, the lineage kept dwindling. And then, at the end of the 1970s, they returned.

In 1978 a pack was sighted in Vittangi, close to the 'three-state cairn' that marks the spot where Sweden, Finland and Norway meet, but the next winter it had mysteriously disappeared. Then, a year later, another pack was sighted in Värmland.

The literal translation of Norrland is 'north land'. But it isn't actually the northern half of the country. It's more like two thirds. Maybe more, if you ask someone from the south. Värmland, the province where *The Saga of Gösta Berling* takes place, is the northernmost region you can find yourself in without being in Norrland. It has all the characteristics of the actual north: wilderness, desolation, and breath-taking mountains, dark green to the point where they look shot through with blackish blue.

In this environment, those resurgent wolves thrived. In 1983 the pack grew: for the first time since the early 1960s, a batch of wolf cubs was born in Sweden. The Värmland pack, now eight members strong, became the first founding family of the new Swedish wolf population. (There's a total of seven founding packs, all of them immigrants walking across the border from Russia and Finland.) By 2009 the wolf population had ballooned to 210. It was decided that numbers in fact needed to be kept down, for the peace of mind of the people that share the land with these beautiful but nonetheless deadly predators. Hunting was allowed for the first time in over forty years. Nonetheless, before the 2016 wolf hunt, there were thought to be as many as 415 wolves in Sweden.

The wolf hunt is considered a preservation of game, a protective hunt, devised to make sure that the packs don't outgrow their territories. During this year's hunt, which began on an icy-cold 2 January, a total of forty-six wolves were licensed to be shot.

You can't just sit and wait for a wolf. First of all, there needs to be snow, preferably the new kind, where even the lightest paws will leave a trace. Once you've found fresh paw prints you can't track the wolf in a straight line — they'll outrun you in two shakes of a lamb's tail. Instead, you need to start making huge circles. If you're able to circle back to where you began without finding an exit trail, you slowly shrink the circle with each lap, until you have the location of the wolf in the middle of the circle. Then you call in the rest of the hunters and drive the wolf in their direction.

Olle, an experienced woodsman and hunter, has organised wolf hunts, but as leader of his team he is never the one who pulls the trigger. He's met them though. 'Once I was going to a part of the woods where I knew a wolf had been sighted recently,' he tells me. 'When I got there I heard him howling in the distance, so I answered. It didn't take him more than ten or twelve minutes to get to me. He stood in front of me, in the middle of the road, glowering at me, and I felt like it was a pair of mean, ugly eyes staring at me. I shouted but he didn't react. Then I started shouting and clapping my hands and he disappeared back into the woods. I turned to walk back to the car and I noticed his mate had been with him. The prints in the snow were parallel to mine: she had been tracking me from behind.'

Olle says that he doesn't feel at all like the wolf is his hunting competitor. He doesn't care if the wolves slay an elk or two. There are plenty of elk for everyone, 'but they take our dogs. And then we can't hunt at all.' His views are shared by a lot of people who live close to wolves. For dog owners and farmers with livestock it gets personal: you don't have to lose very many pets, or come across more than one of your lambs, half-eaten but still alive, in order to dislike wolves for a long time.

Tom Arnbom, a WWF expert on predators, says humans aren't the only ones who fear wolves: wolves are afraid of wolves too. 'When wandering lone wolves enter the territory of another pack, they will start moving at higher speed and keep running until they've exited the territory. Wolves like to keep a distance. That might be what the

1. 2016 WOLF HUNT
—
In January, Swedish authorities gave hunters a temporary licence to cull 36 wolves, nearly 10 per cent of its overall population. Although the issue was referred to Sweden's Super Administrative Court, activists feared that many of the wolves would be killed by the time the case was heard.

REFLECTING
The tranquility of a Swedish lake, as captured by ANDREAS LARSSON. Gösta Berling's adventures take place around a lake named Lovren, based on the real lake Fryken, near the town of Sunne.

THE SAGA OF GÖSTA BERLING

howling is for too: to signal a position, in order to be able to keep a safe distance to other wolves.'

A lone wolf is a wolf that has left his or her birth pack, to search for a mate and a territory of its own. Lone wolves are vagabonds. And they're fast: a wandering wolf can pass several counties in less than a month. One Polish wolf walked to the Netherlands, but the record is held by a Scandinavian wolf who was born in the south-east of Norway and in twenty months walked through the entire country, passing through Sweden and Finland before being legally shot close to the Russian border. Of all the land mammals, only humans have a greater natural spread across the globe than wolves. And, like humans, wolves create strict hierarchies in their packs. For example, only the mother and father wolf are allowed to procreate. The siblings stay kids as long as they live with their birth pack, and a pack usually consists of two to nine members. A pack raises new babies together and hunts together, moving quickly over vast swathes of land. A standard territory is about 1,000 square kilometres.

Unless you live in the woods, or, like Olle, know how to call a wolf, you probably aren't going to see one. Identifying the scats is easy though: wolf scats are filled with frizzy elk hair and lots of white bits. The predators, er, wolf down the entire elk when they eat, and the bones turn into a calcareous mass in their intestines. Sometimes, wolf furs will turn up in certain of the less politically correct second-hand stores in Stockholm. The bristle is coarse and rough, and unlike the wolves in fairy tales, it's not actually grey but urine-coloured, resembling a dirty blond Alsatian.

Colours aside, the old sagas have much to teach us about the Swedish wilderness. Ancient Swedish animistic beliefs include lake spirits, tree spirits and house spirits, all of whom need to be appeased, or else... There's also Bäckahästen, a magnificent white horse that will lure children onto its back and then dive into a stream and drown them. There's Skogsrå, or Huldra, who looks like a pretty lady, but when she turns around her back is a rotted-out tree trunk. There's Näcken, a wildly beautiful young man who plays his violin in the nude, sitting in a brook or by a watermill, but if you listen to his magical songs he'll lure you into the deep and kill you.

Wolves, though, are mostly just wolves, and that's frightening enough. The Christian Church described the wolf as the devil's creation; even the gods of the Vikings, the Æsir, were afraid of Fenrir, the monstrous wolf that roamed Valhalla before the gods managed to bind him with a magical fetter. In *The Saga of Gösta Berling* wolves pursue Gösta and his runaway girlfriend through a wintry Värmland landscape. The latter wonders to herself if there will be anything left of the two of them for people to find. Since they're being chased by twelve wolves, the answer is probably 'no'. Wolf packs will slay the same number of animals every year (120 elk, to be precise), regardless of the size of the pack, the only difference being that the larger packs leave very little biomass — i.e. leftovers — for the rest of the forest's carnivores. With a pack of twelve wolves on your heels, your bones would be gnawed clean.

More recently, black metal has attempted to capture the spirit of the wilderness, and, a bit like the old folk-tales, it doesn't so much show you what the Nordic forest looks like as how it feels. The music

---

2. SCATS
—
By studying the faeces of wolves, scatologists — as such researchers are known — are able to gain information on factors including diet and inbreeding levels.

3. NÄCKEN
—
These shape-shifting water spirits are common in folklore from all Germanic countries; in the English county of Sussex, they are known as 'knuckers'.

THE SAGA OF GÖSTA BERLING

WOLVES
A trio of watchful wolves, as photographed by **BENJAMIN ALEXANDER HUSEBY** in the epic wilds of Scandinavia.

THE HAPPY READER

VÄRMLAND STYLE
A girl in traditional Värmland dress, as photographed using early colour techniques in the 1920s.

manifests the condensed darkness, the cold and the desolation, and turns it into something alluring in its power. Wolves, perpetual outsiders even among other animals, are common symbols. 'It is the magic combination of fierceness and beauty that makes the wolf an exception even in nature,' says Erik Danielsson, of Swedish black metal band Watain. 'Wolves are revered outlaws, feared in their bestial nature, yet also objects of fascination and curiosity, of naturally inhabited and unreachable grace.'

The old farmers would use protective magic against the wolves: cows would be smeared with a mix of tar and valerian root to protect them against both wolves and the aforementioned Huldra. The many words for wolf that exist in the Swedish language offer an insight into our relationship with the creature. The oldest is *ulv*, which is the etymological root of 'wolf'. But *ulv* became magically tainted. People feared that using the animal's true name was like summoning it, and swapped to *varg*, which actually means something along the lines of 'perpetrator of violence'. But as the wolves kept devouring the farmers' livestock, *varg* soon became tainted in the same way as *ulv*, and the synonyms piled up.

Wolves have distinct personalities. Some are so shy that you can tiptoe through their territory without ever knowing that they're watching you. Others show no fear. They become comfortable in villages and backyards and take up a special diet of sheep and hunting dogs. The infamous she-wolf Ylva, who was the result of an incestuous affair within the original Värmland pack, wreaked havoc in northern Värmland in 1987, attacking sixteen dogs and killing four. When she tried to mate with a Swedish elkhound — amazingly caught on camera in the documentary *Vargens väg* — that was the end of Ylva. She was shot shortly after, to prevent the possibility of wolf-dog hybrids. A hybrid is a disaster waiting to happen, because if there's one thing that actually makes a wolf dangerous, it's the loss of fear. (Wolf-dogs exist, but for natural reasons are rare: in the footage it's clear that Ylva feels very conflicted towards the dog.)

The likelihood of actually being chased by wolves is small. But even though, by the time *The Saga of Gösta Berling* was published in 1891, wolf attacks had become a distant memory, that scene still felt terrifyingly plausible to readers. In 1820, the year that Gösta's story begins, there was a series of vicious wolf attacks in Värmland. More than thirty people were attacked. Several children were killed and partially eaten, proving that the wolves responsible weren't rabid, but actually hunting prey. In the end, the Värmland attacks were traced back to a single animal, the Gysinge Wolf. He had been raised by humans, along with his two siblings, at a nearby mansion. When they became troublesome pets, the father of the house took them out to the woods to kill them. But he only managed to kill two of the pups, and set the third one free. When the Gysinge Wolf was killed, the attacks ended, and there haven't been any since.

4. VALERIAN ROOT

Valerian root has long been thought to contain magical properties. Perhaps that is why it's a main ingredient in the Draught of Living Death potion in the Harry Potter series.

5. SMALL

There is a much higher likelihood of being killed by a wasp than by a wolf: wasps kill more people directly than any other animal in Sweden, about one per year.

ELIN UNNES grew up in Norrland, Sweden, the daughter of two hunters. She's never seen a wolf, but has seen wolverines, a lynx, a bear cub and an otter. For many years she was the Nordic Editor of *Vice* magazine while also leading a secret double life as a hobby vegetable gardener. She is working on the follow up to her first book, *The Secret Gardener.*

SOCIETY

In 1909 Selma Lagerlöf won a Nobel Prize, an award that has come to be a repository for our most utopian dreams about the world's future — exactly, writes NICHOLAS LEZARD, like Scandinavia itself.

'THIS IS A HUGE SURPRISE!'

In 1888, Alfred Nobel, a Swedish manufacturer and inventor of modern high-grade explosives, was surprised to read, in a newspaper obituary headed by his own name, the strapline: 'The Merchant of Death Is Dead'. As it turned out, the French newspaper responsible, so the story goes, had confused him with his brother, but it at least raised the question for him as to how he would be remembered. Having sent so many others to an early death, perhaps he was shocked that he, alone, was able to come back from one.

There are various ways in which one could react, from the noble to the ignoble. My pun is intentional, and one wonders how the prize Alfred founded in order to clear the stain of death from his history would have fared had his last name been, say, Johannson. (The most common surname in Sweden, at the time of writing.) Let us agree that he could have done far worse.

Norwegians are involved in the prize as well as Swedes; they had to be, as Norway and Sweden were one country, technically, until 1905. People outside Scandinavia tend to either forget this, or only remember it in honest confusion. But, once recalled, it only helps reinforce the idea that we are seeing the Benign Scandinavian Model replacing the ancient, very un-benign S. M., the one of longboats and rape and pillage. (Yes, I know we are now being invited to rethink that image and see Vikings as peaceful traders, but you know what? That doesn't really wash. Sorry.) And you think I make too much of their heritage, now getting on for a millennium old? Believe me, it persists, and all you need to see to confirm it is the sight of Swedish football fans, en route to or from an international match, wearing plastic Viking helmets as a *de rigueur* adornment to their costume. These fans are, in my experience, utterly harmless, in the nicest way, and the manner in which they have turned around their past to make it completely unthreatening is charming; and we get it.

There are, however, dark undercurrents; there always were, but they are now beginning to bubble up again to the surface. I remember being surprised to read how William Burroughs, holed up in Malmö, found it a worldwide centre, *after the war,* for the propagation of anti-Semitic fascism; and the Swedish and Norwegian record during that conflict is not one inscribed in letters of gold in the history books. Swedish ameliorism, or utopianism, may seem to others, in its rigorous high-mindedness, to hold itself up to ridicule; yet there is nothing wrong behind the impulse, unless it is perhaps to whitewash a history; and at least the violence of Scandinavian history is far enough in the past for no one, apart from me, and that only tongue-in-cheek, to think that this is the case. But my tongue is only half in my cheek; and I can only speculate on what Nobel himself might have been thinking when he saw

6. INVOLVED
—
Alfred Nobel established five prizes in total: Chemistry, Literature, Peace, Physics, and Physiology or Medicine. All are decided by Swedish committees except for the prestigious (and controversial) Peace Prize, which is awarded by the five-strong Norwegian Nobel Committee.

7. LITERATURE PRIZE

Last year's winner of the Nobel Prize in Literature, the Belarusian writer Svetlana Alexievich, was the fourteenth woman to have been awarded the prize. The list in full:

1909 — Selma Lagerlöf
1926 — Grazia Deledda
1928 — Sigrid Undset
1938 — Pearl Buck
1945 — Gabriela Mistral
1966 — Nelly Sachs
1991 — Nadine Gordimer
1993 — Toni Morrison
1996 — Wislawa Szymborska
2004 — Elfriede Jelinek
2007 — Doris Lessing
2009 — Herta Müller
2013 — Alice Munro
2015 — Svetlana Alexievich

the words 'merchant of death' applied to himself. Did he think of his Viking ancestors and say to himself, 'Not again'? I doubt it: he didn't have to. The contemporary carnage was all around him (and about to get immeasurably worse, thanks in part to him), and this was the way to make amends, as honourable as any. (It is worth noting that Nobel's work in explosives was itself inspired by consideration for the safety of those obliged to handle them; and he also invented plywood. Make of that what you will.)

Anyway, here we have it: the most high-minded prize on earth. The judgements of the Nobel Committee are never meaningfully challenged, except, of course, in the fields of Peace, which I'll get on to in a minute, and Literature, but that is because writers are terrible, almost completely without exception, driven by envy and jealousy in ways which scientists can only marvel at. Also, everyone with any middlingly serious interest in the Literature Prize fancies themselves, even if they have yet to write a book of some or any kind, potentially in with a chance for it; it is actually a useful hallmark of delusion, and not just in the ways you might expect, for when you consider that Simenon died baffled and hurt that he had not been summoned to Stockholm, I hope you see how pernicious this idea of the ultimate prize can be, what a maggot in the brain it is; for, at some strange level, he had a point. It is perhaps more uplifting to consider the example of Samuel Beckett, whose wife, when phoned up by the Committee with the news that he had won it, said 'Catastrophe!' (which word became the title of one of his last plays, dedicated to the then-imprisoned Václav Havel, one of the few people who could plausibly have been up for both Literature and Peace prizes) and refused to attend the ceremony itself.

As for the Peace Laureates, here we enter into weird territory, where the origin of the Prize clashes most jarringly against its intention. Literary Laureates may have been harrumphed at — it is debatable, for instance, how much of Winston Churchill's works were even written by him, and the only excuse for his prize anyway, even if he had indeed written every word, was as gratitude for having co-defeated the Nazis, and his being the only world leader with that claim who had actually

It's not just about the nice medal: a Nobel Prize cheque comes in at around $1 million.

THE HAPPY READER

THE OTHER UK

Sweden and Norway were once a single entity: the United Kingdoms of Sweden and Norway ('Sweden-Norway' for short). The pan-Scandinavian union involved a shared monarch and foreign policy, and autonomy in most other things including laws, armies, currencies and state churches. Sweden-Norway came into being in 1814 — Norway reluctantly agreed to the arrangement so as to avoid being conquered by Napoleon — and stayed in place until 1905. It wasn't the only Nordic union: for example, immediately before the United Kingdoms were established, Sweden and Finland were united, and Norway and Denmark were Norway-Denmark.

FLAG
The 'Union mark' of Norway and Sweden combined the flag colours of both kingdoms. It was nicknamed the 'herring salad' – these also being the colours of pickled herring, beetroot and potato.

written anything at the time — but generally, the grumbles are either along the lines of 'we haven't heard of him/her' (it's usually 'him', of course), or 'he' (again) 'isn't that good.' There may be the awkward sense of balances being redressed, or legacies acknowledged — I will only mention as a side-issue the way the Literature Prize is usually a passing bell on a writer's career, often accepted resignedly as such — but there's never been the sense of absolute, astonished horror, as when Kissinger was awarded his in 1973. Anxiety and remorse about Mother Teresa's award may be slow in rising, but to this day and through the ages, the Kissinger award will stand as the high-water mark of false consciousness, or realpolitik, or cognitive dissonance, or wishful thinking, or some point in the Venn diagram where all these attributes meet.

I suppose we ought to be grateful that the one thing the Nobel Committee has never been accused of is corruption, or at least not of any but the most piddling kind, or by conspiracists who entertain complexly organised doubts about Obama's legitimacy. Nineteen seventy-four wasn't one of the great literary years: the Prize then went to two Swedish authors, Eyvind Johnson and Harry Martinson, whom I still haven't heard of; at the time, Greene, Nabokov, Borges and gosh knows who else were all in the running. (Sometimes the recurring snub is as much its own award as the award itself.) And so, year after year, the Nobels do their trick of being the biggest game in town. And as the very idea of Sweden itself begins to collapse, as the thugs and the neo-fascists address themselves to the displaced of darker skin entering among them — Malmö is still a pretty bad place for that kind of thing — we can watch the noble Nobels, the Committee, with their lavish dinners, their unimpeachable and unviolable dignity; their sashes.

NICHOLAS LEZARD is a critic for *The Guardian* and a columnist for *The New Statesman*, and has his Nobel acceptance speech pretty well sewn up.

FOOD & DRINK

It's telling that Gösta Berling's story begins with booze, and booze-related shame. Sweden has a complicated relationship with alcohol, writes TRAVIS ELBOROUGH, one neatly illustrated in the way its citizens can only buy the stuff from idiosyncratic, government-run institutions.

WHERE THE CUSTOMER IS ALWAYS WRONG

Every nation on earth has its own distinctive institutions. Places that are so characteristic of a particular society's way of life that they become emblematic of the country at large. These do, of course, reach the point of hoary old clichés. But who, in all honesty, thinking of France doesn't picture brass-clad bistros and brasseries, for instance? Or, when considering America, conjure up visions of diners and drugstores? Ditto Germany and Bierkellers. Greece and tavernas. Spain and tapas bars. Britain and its draughty, Australian lager-purveying pubs. And if there is anything that is truly emblematic of Sweden,

SYSTEM BOLAGET

It's the corporate face of civic disapproval.

leaving IKEA aside, it may well be its Systembolaget shops.

For those who are unfamiliar with these unique establishments, they are the country's state-run retail outlets for alcohol. Currently instantly recognisable by their lurid logo in budgerigar green and yellow, these shops retain a monopoly on the take-home trade of wine, hard liquor and most beer. Their purpose, as a mission statement on their official website puts it, is 'to minimise alcohol-related problems by selling alcohol in a Responsible Way, without profit motive.' Here, the 'Responsible Way' appears to mean to try and avoid selling any of it at all. Or certainly to make the experience as costly, dreary and difficult as possible.

The modern Systembolaget is uninviting: its layout utilitarian, its decor as antiseptic as a hospital corridor, its opening times inconvenient. A quirk that particularly confuses visitors from the US is a refusal to refrigerate beer or white wine, on the grounds that it might persuade punters to choose those items over alternative beverages.

Even so, buying alcohol there is not as hard as it used to be. Earlier incarnations of the stores, strains of which persist in smaller towns, strove purposely to be completely off-putting. In *Fishing in Utopia*, the British writer Andrew Brown's memoir of living in Sweden in the 1970s, he recalls having to make a ten-mile road trip to his nearest Systembolaget in Kungalv, 'a bleak largely windowless grey concrete building' boasting extensive displays of 'temperance propaganda.' The stock itself was not on show and had to be ordered via a catalogue that resembled 'a bus timetable' and was fetched by 'a pitying assistant' from 'mysterious shelves' in a back room.

Set up in 1955, when Sweden was being transformed into a fiercely egalitarian social democratic society, the Systembolaget were conceived as an enlightened but practical means of curing the issues with alcohol that were believed to have bedevilled its population for nearly two hundred years. Once described as a land of sex, suicide and socialism, Sweden suffers from some of the longest and darkest winters and enjoys the brightest, if shortest, summers, of anywhere on earth. Few people could be more easily forgiven for wishing to blot out the bleakness of those black, black days, while equally the exuberance that greets the bright nights of August, which come and go with the fleeting bitter-sweet intensity of a firework, is hard to put back into the bottle.

In the late eighteenth century, the country entered a period which historians refer to gravely as 'the heyday of Swedish alcoholism', for which the finger of blame is usually pointed at King Gustav III, a generally enlightened, if somewhat absolutist, monarch, who actively encouraged his subjects to drink spirits like never before as a handy way of raising tax revenues. The situation worsened over the next forty years, with drunkenness from home-made moonshine becoming widespread in rural areas. Alcoholism was endemic. Then, the pendulum swung to an equal and opposite position. In 1855, the Swedish Temperance Society successfully campaigned to outlaw home distilling. At around the same time the city of Gothenburg took direct control of its taverns by way of the restrictive so-called 'Gothenburg System'. In 1917, the Swedish government introduced a ration-book scheme for alcohol, which persisted until 1955, at which point they nationalised the country's entire wholesale trade in booze with a single body, the Vin-Och Spritcentralen. Correspondingly, to ensure sensible drinking in the home, it rolled out its father-knows-best foot soldiers: the Systembolaget.

These arrangements were to hold, virtually unaltered, for forty-five years. Their persistence speaks volumes about the country's collective (and collectivist) psyche when it comes to anxieties about drink. In an odd parallel to the scarlet letters that harlots were forced to wear for adultery in Puritan New England, customers at Systembolaget are given bright purple plastic bags for their purchases. The booze buyer must then trudge the streets or the path to their car, practically carrying the shameful mark of alcohol upon their person. Abstemiousness, much like chastity elsewhere, is fundamentally held up as the ideal to which all right-minded people should aspire.

In 2000, the European Union forced Sweden to lift some of its heaviest restrictions on the sale of alcohol. Prices have fallen, as have the numbers of those abstaining completely. A further contributing factor hails from cheap imports following the opening, also in 2000, of the Øresund Bridge. This 16-kilometre marvel of modern civil engineering connects the southern Swedish city of Malmö to Copenhagen, the capital city of Denmark, a country with a historically more relaxed view of drinking, and whose most famous brewers, Carlsberg, first produced the 9% proof tramp-juice lager we know as Special Brew for Winston Churchill in 1950. The strongest beer purchasable in many Systembolaget outlets nevertheless is kept soggily pegged to 3.5%, a gravity almost as watery as the Øresund Sound itself and proving that some rivers have yet to be crossed.

TRAVIS ELBOROUGH's books include *The Vinyl Countdown*, *Wish You Were Here* and *London Bridge in America*. He is married to a Swedish-born American teetotaller but enjoys the odd glass of O.P. Anderson for purely medicinal reasons, obviously.

MUSIC

It's pretty much a rule of physics that when a book's been around as long as *The Saga of Gösta Berling*, it will at some point have been repurposed as a band name. But two bands at the same time? Really? In the bizarre (and potentially infinite) world of musical nomenclature, writes SIMON PRICE, there's no excuse for pillaging the same novel title as someone else.

WHY BANDS HAVE THE MOST RIDICULOUS NAMES

What's in a band name? Arguably, very little, when you consider that the most successful group of all time also had one of the worst names in history. Nobody thinks of the dreadful pun on which it is based, cornier than Green Giant and cheesier than Cheddar, when they hear the words 'The Beatles'. There's a point, in a band's trajectory, above which a name is just a sound that signifies them, and escapes its original meaning entirely. As long as you write a million-selling song or two, you can call yourself pretty much anything.

Lower down the food chain, however, choosing a name can be a vital, life-or-death decision. And one thing it needs, in a crowded and planet-sized marketplace, is to be unusual and, ideally, unique. At the time of writing, two bands on opposite sides of the globe are simultaneously named after Selma Lagerlöf's debut novel.

The instrumental rock band Gösta Berling's Saga were formed in Stockholm in 2000, and are signed to avant-garde indie label Cuneiform. For them, coming from the home of the book, the name is not a particularly left-field choice. 'We were looking for a name,' explains drummer Alexander Skepp, 'that had a feeling to it which was illustrating but not too substantial. We realised that most Swedes had a vague understanding of the novel, which was our starting point, but mostly associate it with the settings described in it — Swedish winter landscapes and demon-driven sleigh rides.'

A decade and a half later, enter Gösta Berling, a post-punk/shoegaze band from Oakland, California, who presumably didn't do any due-diligence googling before naming themselves after the Garbo film, assuming that the chances of someone else being named after a relatively obscure work of Scandinavian fiction were next to nil. Facepalms all round, and a key lesson: it doesn't matter how strange and arcane your band name is — check!

Skepp hadn't heard of his Californian counterparts until approached for this article. 'We probably couldn't care less about it either,' he adds, 'from a confrontational point of view.' However, the American band had, belatedly, become aware of the clash. 'We know of the other band,' says bassist Greg Dubrow, 'and they play a style of music very different from ours, so it's not an issue.'

In the days before search engines, checking wasn't so easy, and you could end up lumbered with ugly geographical appendages to your name. Tim Burgess estimated that during promotional trips to the States, he had to say 'Hi, I'm Tim from The Charlatans UK' 80,000 times when recording radio station idents. If this is an exaggeration by a factor of 400%, that's still enough times to make him believe that The Charlatans UK was his band's real, and somewhat clunky, name. In fact, they'd been forced to add the 'UK' due to a pre-existing San Francisco psychedelic band from the 1960s.

This was a common occurrence in the 80s and 90s, as The English Beat and The Mission UK found out. Crossing the Atlantic in the opposite direction, Kurt Cobain's Nirvana managed to reach a settlement with their English namesakes which allowed both bands to use the same handle. Sometimes, the dry negotiations of music industry lawyers would throw up something oddly pleasing, such as the electro duo whose breakthrough album *Moon Safari* was officially credited to 'Air French Band'. Or, the daddy of them all, The London Suede. It proved mildly ruinous to Suede's career when American jazz-folk singer Suzanne de Bronkart, who had been trading under the same name, took legal action and wouldn't budge. As singer Brett Anderson told biographer David Barnett, 'I've always really enjoyed playing America. I really love playing there. The only thing that stops Suede playing America is the fact we had to change our name. And I couldn't go over there and play under the name The London Suede because I was just too embarrassed by it.' But he's wrong, at least about the name itself. There's something gently psychedelic and surreal about the name The London Suede which plain old Suede just doesn't have.

These days, there's no excuse. Although, to be fair to the Gösta Berling bands, it does

Swedish popsters ABBA took on their acronymous name having grown tired of 'Björn & Benny, Agnetha & Anni-Frid', their mouthful of an early moniker.

seem vanishingly improbable that two bands would go for a name based on that particular novel. It is, after all, hardly topical right now. But topicality itself can be a trap. An easy pitfall is to be short-termist in your thinking, and choose a name that's overly of-the-moment. In 2000, the custody battle for Cuban orphan Elián González inspired satirical news website *The Onion* to run the headline '47 Punk Bands Change Their Name to The Miami Relatives'. (A year later, a no-hoper bar band called The Miami Relatives did turn up in an episode of *The Sopranos*. Either a case of great minds, or someone at HBO having *The Onion* on their browser favourites.)

It's an endlessly adaptable formula. In 2010, during the hunt for a notorious Bradford serial killer, I predicted a glut of heavy metal bands called Crossbow Cannibal. In 2012, during the London Olympics, I made the same remark about Women's Quadruple Skull. In 2013, when a story broke about the USA's use of dirty weapons in Iraq, it was Depleted Uranium and White Phosphorous. (Satisfyingly, I discovered that both those bands did indeed exist.) Most recently, after the 2015 Conservative Party conference, I foresaw at least half a dozen indie bands called Northern Powerhouse. (No sign of one yet, but someone's already bagged the Soundcloud account.)

The power of Google cuts both ways, and can destroy a band's fleeting mystique with a few key-taps. It's always disappointing when a seemingly original name turns out to be lifted wholesale from cult fiction or cinema. You could get away with it in the pre-internet days: as a teenager, I remember pondering the elegant strangeness of the band name Eyeless in Gaza and the Visage single 'The Damned Don't Cry', only to learn later that the former was an Aldous Huxley novel and the latter a 1950 film noir starring Joan Crawford.

My two favourite alternative acts of the 1980s took very different approaches to nomenclature. The Jesus and Mary Chain's name sounded heretical, subversive and, above all, sexy. (And, as far as anyone knows, it was all their own work.) The Smiths, however, couldn't have been plainer if they were a bag of ready salted crisps made by their snack-manufacturer namesake. 'It's the most ordinary name in the universe,' Morrissey told *Smash Hits* at the time. 'We christened the group when many were hiding behind long names like Eyeless in Gaza (there they are again!), or Orchestral Manoeuvres in the Dark. And when you meet these people, they're so ordinary. Some haven't even read a book.' The deliberately drab and glamour-free The Smiths paradoxically became a strength: it was so blank and empty that they filled it with their own colour-palette and personality. Those two words meant them, and only them.

My favourite band of the '90s, Manic Street Preachers, benefited from the Beatles Effect: their name, which reeks of trying too hard when you first read it, is now just a five-syllable noise which, like The Smiths, means the thing to which it refers, and nothing else. Other acts from the same era who didn't exactly trip off the tongue, like David Devant & His Spirit Wife (named after a real Victorian magician) or Gentle Ihor's Devotion (your guess is as good as mine) fell some way short of the household-name status required for that sort of brand familiarity.

Sometimes, necessity is the mother of invention. I've always admired the way the Sensational Alex Harvey Band dealt with the aftermath of their charismatic leader's death. There was something pleasingly honest, on-the-nose and 'exactly what it says on the tin' about their subsequent albums being credited to SAHBWA, or the Sensational Alex Harvey Band Without Alex. Plenty of other veteran acts routinely show no such scruples, touring without the original lead singer, or even with just one (or fewer) original member, but retaining their still-bankable name.

Fashion is also a factor. Trends this millennium have included the dropping of the definite article, hence the Pluralists: bands ending with an 's', but with no 'the' beforehand, e.g. Editors and Foals. Then there was the Irritable Vowel Syndrome epidemic which spawned a rash of consonant-only acts. In the early part of this decade, it was possible to scan the gig listings and see the alphabetically depleted likes of SBTRKT, MGMT, HTRK, BLK JKS, STRFKR, CHLLNGR, PVT, MNDR. (I blamed PRML SCRM.) And then you had the Awkward Squad: bands who didn't have names at all, but instead went with symbols. These included Mercury winners Alt-J (whose triangular computer-key logo was supposedly their real name), whose bright idea could be traced back via early noughties punk-funkers !!!, which we were meant to pronounce 'chk-chk-chk', and Prince's stroppy 'Symbol' phase, to '80s oddballs Freur (an early incarnation of Underworld), whose original name was an unpronounceable squiggle.

The worst trend of all, one which shows no sign of abating, is the Boring Birth-Certificate Crew: the endless deluge of singer-songwriters, from Ed Sheeran to Laura Marling, from James Bay to Jack Garratt, who stick with their given names. If they put so little imagination into their pop persona, what chance for their records? Someone needs to hold a metaphorical pistol to their heads and force them to come up with something — anything — that's more interesting. Tragic Lightning Boy, perhaps, or Airport Rendezvous. You can have those for free.

Just make sure that no one else has got there first.

SIMON PRICE is an award-winning Welsh music journalist and DJ. He has contributed to publications including *Melody Maker*, *The Independent On Sunday*, *The Guardian* and *Q*, written a best-selling biography of Manic Street Preachers, and DJed for artists ranging from AC/DC to Pharrell Williams. His favourite Swedish band name is either Crucified Barbara or The Leather Nun.

Selma's cavaliers are constantly playing the Swedish card game *kille*. And even for those of us who didn't spend our childhoods playing it in lakeside summer homes, writes NAOMI ALDERMAN, it's hard not to become transfixed by the cards' tarot-like faces.

NEVER-ENDING PLAYTIME

In his short novel — or long short story — *Chess*, Stefan Zweig tells the story of 'Dr. B' who succumbs to a case of 'chess poisoning'. Having been imprisoned by the Gestapo in a cell that is comfortable but contains nothing to read or write with, Dr. B comes into possession of a book of chess problems. He's never been interested in chess, but this book is the only thing he has to occupy his mind. Soon, chess consumes his waking days, and his sleep too. Eventually, he sees everything in his life through the prism of chess: 'I could think only in terms of chess, only in chess moves, chess problems; sometimes I would wake with a damp brow and become aware that a game had unconsciously continued in my sleep, and if I dreamt of persons it was exclusively in the moves of the bishop, the rook, the advance and retreat of the knight's move.'

We who have played video games have also experienced this curious malady — even without the Gestapo forcing it on us. I've played games for hours, for days, until the point that when I closed my eyes the games continued to unspool endlessly. Diablo II — a game I played for at least four hours a day for several months — left knights slaying demons inside my eyelids every night as I reached for sleep. At such times, one can't help wondering what one has ended up *doing* to one's brain by incessant games-playing. I don't like that state. When I play games now, I try never to reach it.

The figures in games provide a pleasing mathematical abstraction of real life; only certain elements of life exist in them, often battle but maybe also orderly matching (patience, poker), acquisitive capitalism (Monopoly), the forces of chance (snakes and ladders). Games have

8. IN TERMS OF CHESS
—
This story has certain parallels with the real life experience of Natan Sharanksy, who spent nine years in Soviet prisons, half of which was served in solitary, having been accused of being a US spy. A onetime chess prodigy, he later described playing thousands of games in his head to pass the time. Unlike Dr. B, chess didn't drive him insane — it kept him sane.

THE SAGA OF GÖSTA BERLING

KILLE CARDS
Cuckoos and pigs are high-ranking cards in this hilarious and fun card-swapping game.

their meanings — and often codify systems of value we've otherwise discarded (as it were). Playing cards contain a certain symbolism about feudal life: there will be unnamed people of various statuses from the lowly ones to the high-value tens, but above them are the noblemen jacks, then the queen and then, always on top, the kings. Each pack is a court in miniature, with the ace or perhaps the joker serving as the fool — the one who is both high and low, the possibility of revolution. One wonders what the constant reshuffling of that old system *does* to us.

In this context, what can one make of the Swedish game of *kille*? Its cards include the familiar-feeling: the numbers 1 to 12, the knight, the harlequin. But also more surreal additions: the hussar, the inn, the flowerpot, the mask, the pig, the wreath, the cuckoo. The game mostly involves swapping cards — but if you try to swap with someone who's holding some of the 'face cards' there are other rules. It sounds like a game Borges characters might play in a labyrinth. For me, its opacity underlines the foreignness even of that which seems familiar. The mid-nineteenth century doesn't feel so long ago. Sweden doesn't feel so far away. But this game? Trying to swap a flowerpot for a pig is as inexplicable as the number of women who fall for Berling himself.

NAOMI ALDERMAN is an award-winning novelist and videogame creator. Her novels include *Disobedience* and *The Liars' Gospel*. She is co-creator and lead writer of the hit smartphone audio adventure *Zombies, Run!* Penguin will publish her new novel, *The Power* — about a world where women are physically more powerful than men — in November.

ICON

In 1924, a movie adaptation of Lagerlöf's novel was not only a surprise international hit but launched the career of one of the most important film stars ever to have lived. YELENA MOSKOVICH investigates the strange and secretive life of the Swedish actress Greta Garbo.

FABRICATING GARBO

'The Screen's Great Sufferer', as described in her obituary in *The New York Times* in 1990, Greta Garbo and her mystic face loomed over Hollywood's Golden Age, a cult libido for both men and women. She was the highest-paid actor or actress at MGM for most of her career, starring in an endless string of cinematic *chef d'œuvres* such as *Grand Hotel*, *Anna Karenina*, *Camille*, *Ninotchka*. The King of Sweden made her a Commander of the Swedish Order of the Polar Star. The Guinness Book of Records named Garbo 'the most beautiful woman who ever lived.'

But in the wake of the Second World War, after twenty-eight films, at the age of thirty-five, the world's most in-demand persona announced she would be entering a 'temporary' retirement. Despite propositions from Alfred Hitchcock and Ingmar Bergman, even Jean Cocteau, who had written the part of Elisabeth in *Les Enfants Terrible*

THE SAGA OF GÖSTA BERLING

GRETA AS ELIZABETH
Mauritz Stiller's movie adaptation of Lagerlöf's epic tapestry of tales saw one of the novel's main romantic threads promoted to the status of central storyline. Greta Garbo portrays the young and beautiful Countess Elizabeth Dohna. Gösta Berling, played by Lars Hanson, is her tutor. The two fall in love; adventures ensue.

with her in mind, Garbo retreated from the public eye and did not do another film.

The strict privacy she insisted upon only intensified her allure. Anne Frank pinned a cut-out of Garbo's face onto her wall in the annex. Hitler sent her fan-mail. The media frantically reported on why she wouldn't marry — especially with proposals from stars such as John Gilbert — why she refused to give interviews, or autograph photos, or answer fan-mail, why she kept in disguise and under alias. The psychiatrist Dr Louis E. Bisch, relying on his medical expertise to de-mystify the Swedish Sphinx, concluded that she was 'harboring a powerful father complex', and it was this that gave Garbo her irresistible sex appeal. Freudian bullying became public opinion: her assertiveness regarding her career and private life must surely be cruxed on some psychotic lack of male. But Garbo would not be bullied. The Great Sufferer refused to suffer publicly. It may have been the film that launched her career back in Sweden, when she was only seventeen, which planted the seed for such rebellion: the adaptation of Selma Lagerlöf's *The Saga of Gösta Berling*, directed by Mauritz Stiller.

Born in 1905 in the lower-working-class Söder district of Stockholm, Greta Lovisa Gustafsson — not yet Garbo — had always dreamed of becoming an actress. She had her father's face: a slight cleft in the chin, a thin-lipped curve of a mouth and sombre eyes. She was deemed plump, clumsy and masculine. Despite his drinking problem, her father warmly and consistently encouraged her. When he became too ill and too drunk for work, Greta, at fourteen, dropped out of school to take care of him. Bedridden in his liquored sleep, Greta read to him. Selma Lagerlöf was one of their mutual favourites. 'If dead things love... I would like to possess their love.'

His kidneys collapsed the following year. He was forty-eight. Greta later recalled, 'For a time after his death I was fighting an absurd urge

> **9. SÖDER**
> —
> Short for Södermalm, the neighbourhood of Söder was originally farmland used to support the city of Stockholm. These days, life in the neighbourhood is less rural and more action packed, even serving as the home of Lisbeth Salander in Stieg Larsson's popular *Millennium* trilogy.

After disappearing from public view Garbo almost became just a regular citizen of Manhattan, where she lived at 450 East Fifty-second Street until her death in 1990. This sighting took place in 1974.

to get up in the night and run to his grave to see that he had not been buried alive.' After a year of small jobs to help support the family, she auditioned for the Royal Swedish Dramatic Theatre Academy: 'There's no blood in my veins, there is only tears!' Her chosen monologue was taken from Lagerlöf's *The Fledgling*. When the jurists stopped her in the middle of her presentation, she ran off stage, almost fainting, sure they didn't want her. Three days later, she received a call. She had been accepted, with a scholarship, and on her sixteenth birthday, she entered the academy.

Soon, this peculiar teenager with a hunched glare and a husky voice caught the eye of Mauritz Stiller, who, with his tantric eyes and wedge moustache, was passing himself off as a world-renowned German film-maker. In fact he was a Polish Jew from Helsinki, fleeing the Tsar's draft. Having charmed the Swedish artistic elite with his finely tailored British suits, custom-made canary-yellow sports car and avant-garde chauvinism, he barked out orders and coughed stylistically, to hide his lingering tuberculosis.

Stiller hand-picked Greta from the academy for his upcoming film adaptation of the quintessential Lagerlöf novel *The Saga of Gösta Berling*, for the role of Elizabeth Dohna, the young married countess who falls for the defrocked priest Gösta Berling. Against the author's objections, Stiller restructured the story with his newly discovered protégée as the centrepiece. She was to be sculpted into his feminine ideal — the 'super-sensual, spiritual, and mystic woman'.

He put Greta on a strict diet to lose twenty pounds and gave her a new surname, Garbo, whose alleged origin is the Polish word *wygarbowac*, 'to tan leather', thus branding her with his 'desire to shape her psychic hide'. Her name was legally changed a month after shooting started. The rumours began — she seventeen, he forty. Though Stiller was a known homosexual, the cast and crew remarked that he was having 'mental, not physical sex with Garbo'. Greta listened devotedly to his every critique. 'I always had a complex because I had so little schooling...'

Stiller, who was described in the industry as 'a sadist in the artistic way', mocked and jolted her publicly during filming, pointing out her 'goalpost walk', her unusually large feet, ungraceful mannerisms and utter lack of skill. He named everything she ate, insisting she ought to eat nothing at all. Sleepless and shaky one day during filming, the usually mild-tempered Greta stopped mid-scene and screamed straight at Stiller, 'I HATE YOU!'

Though rough with the girl named Greta, Stiller was obsessively delicate with the icon named Garbo. He supposedly ordered certain actors to wear large boots to make her feet look smaller. Julius Jaenzon, Sweden's premier cinematographer, was hired to give his full attention to the lighting and framing of Garbo's face. By then she had developed an eye-twitch, possibly because of Stiller's directing style, for which the camera had to be sped up to counterbalance the scrutiny of close-ups.

Despite Stiller's tight grasp, journalist Inga Gaate sneaked in an interview with her during filming. Greta began with rehearsed praise for Stiller, but soon veered into nervous admittances, such as 'being feminine is a lovely quality which I may not have very much of.' Right after the interview, Greta panicked and begged Gaate not to use what she had said. Gaate printed everything. When Stiller got hold of the article,

10. SMALLER

Garbo's feet were mysterious. Although she was rumoured to have big, unattractive feet, this was denied by both her cobbler, Salvatore Ferragamo, and the actor David Niven, who described them as, 'beautifully shaped and long, in correct proportion to her height.'

he became irate, ordering that she remain silent and unresponsive to all press from that point on. He would speak on her behalf.

The final version of *Gösta Berling* was nearly four hours long and had to be premiered in two showings in March 1924 at Roda Kvarn Theatre in Stockholm. Stiller escorted Garbo to both premieres. Lagerlöf only attended one, which some said was due to her bad hip and heavy limp, though most saw it as a protest. The two women were briefly introduced. Teenage Garbo peered nervously at Miss Lagerlöf, an established and revered female writer in the macho profession, quite openly homosexual, confident, authentic, a childhood idol. Stiller pulled Garbo away before they could speak.

Swedish critics echoed the author's disappointment, labelling the film 'a beautifully staged failure'. However, it was distributed in twenty-eight countries, and became a hit in Copenhagen, Helsinki and Berlin, where at the Mozartsaal Theatre it received 'a thunderous ovation'. Stiller gave a speech from his box. He gripped Garbo's wrist and pulled her into the spotlight. She parted her lips and lifted the muscles in her cheeks — it wasn't quite a smile. It was the beginning of her stardom. It was during this trip that Louis B. Mayer from MGM crossed paths with Stiller and his star, eventually signing Garbo to America's most glamorous film studio — and then getting her to lose the rest of the weight.

In Hollywood, Stiller was pushed aside by industry tycoons with greater finances and deeper narcissism. He returned to Sweden, where he passed away at the age of forty-five, most likely from his lifelong untreated tuberculosis. Upon hearing the news, Greta was both devastated and liberated. 'It was a love-hate affair. At times he loved me as much as I hated him.'

After Stiller's death, she began to assert clearer boundaries to ensure confidentiality on her own terms. While MGM and the media insisted on controlling Garbo, Greta guarded her autonomy by communicating through aliases: 'M-Boy' or 'Mountain-Boy' for when she felt masculine and tender, 'Eleanor' when she felt flirty, and 'Miss Cornell', the hypersensitive sociophobe who 'does not like strangers'.

She developed codenames for her lovers as well, referring to Spanish-American writer Mercedes de Acosta, one alleged lover, as 'Black and White'. Rumours spread about affairs with actresses such as Lilyan Tashman and Fifi D'Orsay. Louise Brooks bragged openly about a night spent with the Divine Woman. Garbo denied everything.

In a letter to Marlene Dietrich, de Acosta wrote that she saw 'the real person — a Swedish servant girl with a face touched by God — only interested in money, her health, sex, food, and sleep. And yet her face tricks my mind and my spirit builds her up into something that fights with my brain. I do love her [...] but I have built up in my emotions a person that does not exist.'

Garbo travelled freely and abundantly. Nostalgic for the streets of Stockholm, the sound of her native language, and the ruminative Scandinavian spirit, she often made trips back to Sweden. She came to visit the grave of her father, that of her older sister Alva who had died early of cancer, even the grave of Stiller. But there was one other lingering curiosity, for one of the defining authors of her childhood and the woman whose novel had inadvertently launched her career. By then, Selma Lagerlöf had also become careful with her public image. Amidst

11. DE ACOSTA
—
Mercedes de Acosta's poetry, novels and plays were never particularly successful. What fame she did gain was largely down to a string of affairs with culturally significant figures, including both Dietrich and Garbo. Although her relationship with Garbo fizzled out during the '60s, someone claimed to have spotted the actress, disguised in dark glasses, at the fringes of de Acosta's funeral in 1968.

12. STOCKHOLM
—
In 2015, Stockholm was ranked the world's 'third most reputable city'.

Selma Lagerlöf was the first non-mythological woman to appear on a Swedish banknote. She was recently replaced by Astrid Lindgren as the face of the 20-kronor note, in a currency redesign that saw Greta Garbo become the face of the 100.

the growing Nazi epidemic she was organising the safe refuge of Jewish intellectuals, like Nelly Sachs, to Sweden. In the summer of 1935, Garbo dropped by Lagerlöf's home in Mårbacka uninvited, but the ailing writer happened to be in the hospital at Karlstad. The next year when visiting Stockholm, however, she received a formal invitation from Miss Lagerlöf for tea at her partner Valborg Olander's apartment on Karla Street.

When Lagerlöf opened the door, she stood as Selma, without pretense, looking with warm eyes at the undercover figure before her. Garbo, in her low-brimmed hat and sunglasses, extended a bouquet of flowers but did not say a thing. Selma welcomed her into the drawing room, where Garbo slid off her disguise and took a seat, now a barefaced and tense Greta. The author reached over and patted her sympathetically on the knee, telling her that she had done good work in *Gösta Berling*. At her touch, Greta burst out in a voice that was too loud for the room, 'To think that I'm sitting here with Selma Lagerlöf!'

The two women waded into a conversation, speaking cautiously of Stiller, then Hollywood, the international press, Selma's health, film and literature. Selma even slipped in some business, hinting at film companies in America who might be interested in adapting her novels. Then both women settled into a Nordic silence. Selma, with her limp leg resting in front of her, perhaps contemplating the political climate; Greta, with her painted lips and foreboding stare, retreating into memories of other cherished books, like those of her favourite poet, Harriet Löwenhjelm: 'Sorrow fills the world with ache / All that's gold is mostly fake.'

Selma showed Greta out and she went back to America under her favourite alias, Harriet Brown. The author later recalled that Miss Garbo had 'beautifully sorrowful eyes'. Selma Lagerlöf would pass away a month before Nazi troops pierced into Scandinavia, invading Denmark and Norway in April 1940. In New York, Greta continued to live in resolute anonymity. The disgruntled press began to speculate that Miss Garbo was a spy.

13. MÅRBACKA
—
Lagerlöf grew up in this farmhouse near the town of Sunne, and, years later, her family having long since moved out, she bought it back: it remains open as a de facto museum to the author. *Mårbacka* is also the title of the first volume of her three-part autobiography.

YELENA MOSKOVICH is a Ukrainian-born American author living in Paris. Her debut novel is *The Natashas* (Serpent's Tail 2016). She last visited Garbo's grave, at the Skogskyrkogården Cemetery, in August 2010.

THE HAPPY

DIP
It's amazing how in a country so ardently northern, people still love to skinny-dip (for more Swedish visions by LINA SCHEYNIUS, see pages 33 and 34).

LETTERS

This season the ever-surprising Happy Reader letter box contained messages about expensive shoes, Renaissance magic, and other curious mysteries.

Dear Happy Reader,

I was intrigued by Clancy Martin's tale of consumption at 90s-era Barneys (p36, *THR5*). Having only known the store in its later, less streamlined incarnation, I can see how the tight selection of 'maybe fifteen pairs of Manolo Blahniks to choose from' would be, if you were in the market for such a thing, just the right amount of pairs. But this part confused me: 'I learned there that you should be able to balance a proper woman's shoe on the tip of your finger, effortlessly.'

Could someone please talk me through the logistics of this? (Is the toe of the shoe on your pointer finger, and the heel on your palm?). I have one pair of Manolo Blahniks from a former life gathering dust in my closet. Each time I go Marie Kondo-ing, I eye them accusingly. Any opportunity to justify their real estate (They do party tricks! Watch me balance them on my finger!), would be welcome.

    Best,
    Elisabeth Fourmont
    Paris, France

Dear Happy Readers,

A chance encounter with *THR5* meant that my period of gluttonous festive consumption was bolstered by a deeper appreciation of the ways and whyfores of the shops that I had spent the previous month battling through. I was left wondering: why is it that, amongst all the delights that department stores stock, so few of them attempt to sell books? A conundrum perhaps worthy of Zola.

    Yours &c
    Rishi Dastidar
    Kennington, UK

Dear Editor,

On the subject of faux books (p5, *THR5*), I'd like to share some things: firstly, a recommendation for a bizarre YouTube tutorial by Lauren Conrad which shows her cutting the spines from real books to the sound of gentle guitar music and gluing them onto storage boxes where she suggests one can keep scarves.

Secondly, on noticing the abundance of probably unread academic books lining the shelves in London member's club Shoreditch House last week (similar, I thought, to your 'cheap romance paperbacks ironically arranged in the hipster cafe'), this reader would like you to know that a copy of *Eros and Magic in the Renaissance* by Ioan P. Couliano was rescued from neglect and taken home to join a lovingly-arranged bookshelf.

    Yours,
    M. Taylor
    London, UK

Dear Seb,

I enjoyed Gert Jonkers' interview with Buy Nothing Day's founder Kalle Lasn (p49, *THR5*). I found it quite ironic that the credit card charge for my *Happy Reader* subscription renewal was recorded on Buy Nothing Day as I had made a conscious decision to honour the day with no shopping!

    Theresa Keatinge
    Arvada, Colorado, USA

Send thoughts on the magazine and/or Books of the Season to letters@thehappyreader.com or The Happy Reader, Penguin Books, 80 Strand, London WC2R 0RL. If yours makes the issue we'll send you a free copy of next Season's Book.

JOIN THE CLUB

With each issue based around a single classic title, The Happy Reader is Penguin's seasonal, magazine-based book club. The easiest way to be part of it, and receive the latest copy promptly no matter where in the world you live, is to subscribe: simply visit thehappyreader.com to sign up. Subscriptions are just £8 per year in the UK, £12 in Europe or £17 in the rest of the world.

AND BE HAPPY

The next Book of the Season — from which the summer issue will take its inspiration — is Virginia Woolf's extraordinary novel *Mrs Dalloway*.

It's a summer's day in London in the 1920s. A woman named Clarissa Dalloway is planning a party for her husband. As the hours pass, we follow her thoughts, from merry considerations regarding the coming evening (what kinds of flowers shall I buy?) to profound plunges into the terrain of memory and its most painful subcategory, regret — for loves lost, for paths taken, for paths not taken. Despite her seemingly charmed life, she is apparently suffering an existential crisis. As — elsewhere in London — is a man named Septimus Smith, a shell-shocked First World War veteran; Mrs Dalloway doesn't know Mr Smith, but before the day is over she will hear word of him, and it will affect her deeply. Meanwhile, Peter Walsh, an old flame who once proposed to her, is also in town.

Unputdownable and unforgettable, *Mrs Dalloway* ranks as one of the most important novels of the twentieth century — an insightful study of the way in which, in the life of the mind, past, present and future all blur into one.

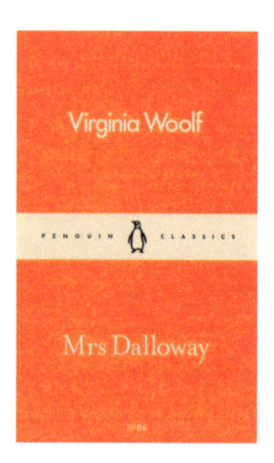

Contemporary jacket design for *Mrs. Dalloway*, originally published in 1925.